The Operations Advantage

Business success beyond sales

AF583311

Tonya Odio

Copyright © 2025 by Executive Foundations

All rights reserved.

No part of this publication may be reproduced, distributed, or transmitted in any form or by any means, including photocopying, recording, or other electronic or mechanical methods, without the prior written permission of the author, except in the case of brief quotations used in critical reviews and certain other noncommercial uses permitted by copyright law.

For permission requests, write to:

Tonya Odio

contact@ef-team.com

First Edition

Cover design by Laura Hammond

Interior design by Mustafijur Rahman

Editing and writing collaboration by Steve Fales

ISBN:

979-8-9986610-0-6 (Ebook)

979-8-9986610-2-0 (Paperback)

979-8-9986610-1-3 (Hardback)

Printed in the United States of America

Disclaimer: The information in this book is provided for general informational purposes only and reflects the author's personal experiences and professional opinions. It is not intended as legal, financial, or business advice. Readers should consult with their own advisors before making decisions based on the content of this book. Brand and product names are trademarks or registered trademarks of their respective owners. The author and publisher disclaim any liability arising directly or indirectly from the use of this book.

Scriptures marked NIV are taken from the NEW INTERNATIONAL VERSION (NIV):

Scripture taken from THE HOLY BIBLE, NEW INTERNATIONAL VERSION

®.Copyright© 1973, 1978, 1984, 2011 by Biblica, Inc.™.

Used by permission of Zondervan

Contents

Dedication

To the entrepreneurs and small business owners ...

This book is dedicated to you.

To those who wake up every day and choose to keep building, even when the path is unclear, the resources are tight, and the weight feels heavy.

You create more than services and products, you create opportunities, jobs, and futures. You carry the pressure, solve the problems, and keep showing up, even when no one sees the fight behind the scenes.

Your ingenuity, grit, and perseverance lay the foundation for others to pursue their own dreams. You are the heartbeat of our communities and the architects of possibility.

Thank you.

A Word from the Author

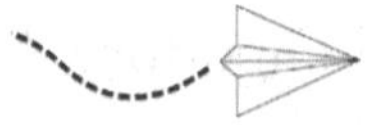

As a business owner, what would you say is the key to a company's success? I'm going to guess your answer is "Sales." After all, without sales there is no company, right? Yet many businesses fail, not because of a fundamental lack of sales, but due to other factors.

Consider these topics, for example:

- *How are you going to acquire customers?* Without a steady stream of new business, today's sales could be the end of the line.
- *How will you provide the firm's services or products?* Sales that are not fulfilled with excellence can be a company's downfall.
- *Where will customer data be stored, and will it be secure?* A data breach ruins a company's reputation, perhaps beyond repair.
- *What practices will govern pricing, invoicing, and collections?* Simply selling without proper support is not adequate for an organization's survival.
- *How will you determine if the business is profitable?* Cash flow from sales is only part of the equation. It's what's left after production and overhead costs that counts most.
- *Will team members know what's expected of them, and what they can expect from their employment?* Inefficiencies, poor communication, unhappy employees, etc. can cost a company thousands.

These issues and more are addressed within well-crafted operational systems, which is exactly what this book is about. While "sales" are indeed important, "operations," from start to finish, are equally critical, if not more so.

How to Use this Book

After presenting some basics in Chapters 1 and 2, I immediately discuss operational procedures around accounting and inventory management. That's because I believe finances and physical resources impact everything a company does. But you don't have to start reading there. Feel free to review the Table of Contents and go straight to the area which interests you most or addresses your biggest pain point.

My Hope for You

This book spells out the definitions, benefits, practical steps, and best practices of business operations, which give every company an advantage over thinking only about sales. No matter where you are in your company's journey, my desire is for you to find that "aha" moment in these pages, and—through application—discover the freedom to grow to the next level.

Sincerely,

Tonya Odio

Founder, Executive Foundations LLC

Author, *The Operations Advantage: Business success beyond sales.*

Acknowledgments

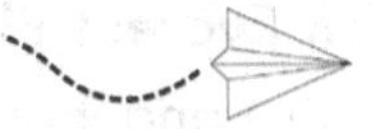

This book would not have been possible without the incredible people who have poured into my life, especially throughout my career and entrepreneurial journey.

Steve Fales, Consultant and Mentor: Thank you for believing in me even more than I believed in myself, and for taking leaps of faith through employment, partnership, and now as editor and collaborator on my first published book. I'm grateful for many things, but a few in particular have been pivotal to the success of Executive Foundations: your role in reconnecting me with Steve Breitkreuz, who now coaches me on this journey; my first client and another one are a result of our relationship; and your suggestion to attend Epic Networking where I not only met Bryan Daly but so many great business connections. Your mentorship and friendship have shaped my life far beyond business, I am forever indebted to you.

Steve Breitkreuz: Thank you for generously sharing your time to coach me on this entrepreneurial journey. Your support has made the path less lonely, and every conversation brings valuable insights. I'm truly grateful to have you in my corner.

Bryan Daly: Thank you for your leadership. Before joining Epic Networking, the idea of networking made me anxious, but your example has completely changed my perspective. Now it's one of the parts of entrepreneurship I enjoy most.

Subject Matter Experts for this book:

- **James Estep with Everest Financial Advisors:** Thank you for your expertise and input on the financial content in this book. I'm especially grateful for your support in my entrepreneurial journey as a trustworthy advisor in both business and personal finance, answering endless questions, and referring the second client to Executive Foundations. Your insight and encouragement mean a great deal.
- **Iris Culp with IC Growth:** Thank you for your input and expertise on the HR content in this book. Your generosity in offering support simply made by a mutual connection truly meant a lot. Your insight helped shape key improvements around HR compliance and strengthened the guidance offered to small business owners. These contributions were invaluable.
- **Earl Spiegel with PEO/Employee Leasing Options:** Thank you for your expert input on the PEO solutions content in this book and for introducing me to Iris Culp. Additionally, collaborating with you on clients in need of PEO services has been a rewarding experience, and I truly appreciate the partnership. You embody the go-giver spirit of entrepreneurship—always looking for ways to benefit both your clients and your network.

Mary Kay Cosmetics: This is where I learned to step out of my comfort zone and overcome my fear of selling. Surrounded by inspiring women and driven by passion for the products, I gained the confidence to do what once felt impossible, such as approaching strangers to share the Mary Kay opportunity.

To all the employers throughout my career: Thank you for the opportunities, challenges, and lessons along the way. Every role taught me something new about business, about people, and about myself. I discovered what I excel at, what I struggle with, and how to grow through both. Each experience, whether smooth or messy, has shaped the professional I am today, and for that I'm deeply grateful.

Family & Friends: Your support and belief in me no matter what I was up to throughout my entrepreneurial journey is priceless. Whether you've supported me through words of encouragement or as a customer, your love has made all the difference. I am deeply grateful for each of you.

And above all, I give glory and thanks to my **Lord and Savior, Jesus Christ**. You are the author of all that is good in my life, and I am simply walking out the story You've already written.

Introduction

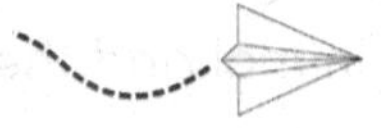

Imagine a day in the future when all your company's operational systems are in place and running smoothly. You know exactly how much revenue the company is generating, and what percentage goes to production expenses and overhead, giving you a clear picture of your profit. The inventory numbers in your computer are accurate, and you never order too much of anything—nor do you run out.

Leads are never overlooked or missed and all your customers are serviced in a timely manner. Orders are processed promptly, and you are on top of your customers' needs before they even reach out for help. Management has full visibility into customer inquiries, so they can ensure clients are receiving the highest level of care. Any negative feedback is addressed to the satisfaction of the unhappy customer, turning him or her into a fan.

There are no missed messages, calls, emails, or chats. All communication is documented properly and visible to relevant team members. Messages from colleagues, clients, prospects, vendors, and salespeople are followed up in accordance with set urgency levels and protocols, keeping production moving with no bottlenecks. As a result, your customers rave about your service.

Team members have clear expectations for completing projects accurately, timely, and within budgets. Management knows exactly how a project is progressing and the status of all deliverables.

Documents are easily retrieved and shared as needed. Information Technology (IT) glitches are addressed with no data losses. Disruptions are minimal and the team is able to continue working through any that do occur.

Marketing efforts generate a consistent flow of leads. Printed and digital materials, including the company's website, are branded accurately, and any changes are quickly updated across both internal documents and external collateral. Everyone understands the organization's brand story and embraces it. In fact, you often hear employees effectively talking about the company's vision, mission and values, as well as its products and services.

None of this happens by accident. It's all by design and part of business operations. But too often, entrepreneurs start out with an idea for a product or service without knowing how to turn that dream into reality. Operations aren't formally addressed until the company has added team members or is ready to scale. These owners attempt to develop systems as they go, with minimal planning or analysis while at the same time trying to do business and keep customers happy. It's action by necessity.

While messy effort is better than no effort, at some point a business needs a more formal structure for operations in order to be sustainable. And the earlier the better, before the situation gets out of control. Well organized systems provide a business with the many benefits outlined in Chapter 1. Setting up these systems for each area of the company requires thoughtful evaluation and time investment to determine the what, who, and how.

That can feel overwhelming, but it doesn't have to be. This book itself provides guidance to alleviate any anxiety you may have about getting started. I further recommend involving others with operational experience or strengths in line with the current state of your business.

A company with efficient business operations will have a set of tools and standard operating procedures in its arsenal. For example, a simple, yet complete Organizational Chart shows everyone's areas of responsibility, to whom they report, and who reports to them, even if the company is lean and people have more than one role. This eliminates confusion and adds a huge dose of peace to everyone's understanding of where they stand in the organization.

Workflow Charts provide team members with clear direction for every business process, creating consistency and virtually zero errors caused by missing a step. An Operations Manual and Employee Handbook define the company's expectations of its employees and lets associates know all the good things they can expect from the company. Later chapters of this book will discuss each of these tools and more.

Sound good? Keep reading as we journey together to our destination of effective and organized operational systems. This book is designed to help you get there from wherever your company stands today.

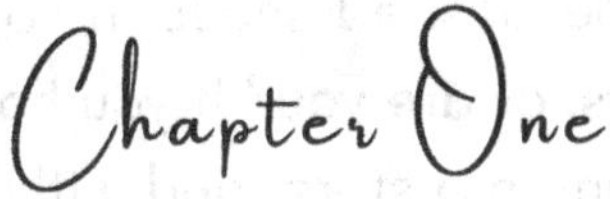

Understanding Operational Systems

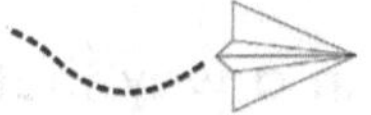

What is an Operational System?

Welcome to your first step in business operations: understanding operational systems. Although the two phrases sound similar, there is a fundamental difference. In this chapter, we'll look specifically at operational systems.

The term "business operations" is used to encompass a number of operational systems within a company. In other words, business operations are made up of several individual operational systems, each of which manage a piece of what your company does, whether you provide a product, a service, or both—and no matter how simple or complex.

Operational systems cover everything involved in the day-to-day activities of business. It's how you get things done internally with the team, and externally for clients/customers, detailing all the steps which take place before the sale, throughout the sales process, as the order is fulfilled, and beyond.

A successful brand is more than a story, it is the fulfillment of that story. If a company says they make shopping pleasurable, they need the right operational systems. Otherwise, the chances of making good on that promise are slim.

When you walk into a shoe store, you probably aren't thinking about all the systems the shop owner has, or should have, so you can easily locate the desired shoes in your size. You are just enjoying the benefits, or are you? If you have ever been unable to find what you want in a store, and without a sales associate in sight, you might merely blame it on terrible customer service. But it goes deeper. Customer service starts with business operations.

The store wasn't set up in a way that made it easy to identify where to find a particular item. This could be poor labeling, a disorganized layout, lack of clear aisles or store flow, items misplaced, or all the above. (I'm stressed just picturing this ... how about you?) Not having an associate available to guide the shopper might be the result of poor hiring, scheduling, training, and/or supervision. All these factors rely on clear systems to support a positive shopping experience. That store will not only lose those who come in, but also potential customers who hear about this negative experience. Effective business operations are of utmost importance.

Software support is another example. It is hugely time-consuming and frustrating to try to get a problem solved when you have to search for ways to contact the company, only to discover they limit customer interaction. Online chat or a phone number allowing access to a knowledgeable human is optimal. Email support is ok but not ideal if there is an urgent need. Each of these customer support functions will follow an established operational system. Thankfully, some software companies do it right.

The most successful businesses have operational systems which are not only effective, but also streamlined. These companies are the most organized and efficient. They have mastered the necessary balancing act of maximizing resources so the client or customer receives the best service possible while keeping the company profitable. My goal throughout this book is to help you do exactly that.

Benefits of Organized Operational Systems

Organized operational systems allow businesses to operate smoothly, respond effectively to challenges, and deliver value. Here are some benefits to having organized operational systems in place:

- *Improved Efficiency:* Employees work more efficiently when they know exactly what needs to be done and how to do it. This saves time and money by having tasks completed by fewer people more quickly and on time.
- *Enhanced Productivity:* Employees can focus on more productive tasks without wasting time searching for information or figuring out how to complete their work, which allows them to focus on efforts which actually move the needle. Clear workflows also prevent bottlenecks and delays.
- *Better Communication:* Defined roles and responsibilities mean employees know who to approach for specific matters. There is less confusion when people are clear on who is handling what. This also helps reduce those unnecessary email chains where people are copied on messages that don't pertain to them.
- *Optimized Resource Allocation:* Organized workflows make it easier to tell where resources are needed most or might be underutilized. Essentially, you can then stop wasting money and provide additional support as needed.

- *Higher Quality Standards:* Consistent processes means fewer mistakes, plus better products and services for customers.
- *Increased Flexibility and Adaptability:* Businesses with organized systems are able to adapt to unexpected challenges or changes in the market. They have clear insights on how they operate and can spend more time on solutions rather than crisis management.
- *Improved Customer Satisfaction:* Customers benefit from quicker response times, accurate information, and reliable service delivery, which creates satisfaction and loyalty.
- *Cost Savings:* Companies save money with processes which eliminate redundant work.
- *Compliance and Risk Management:* Clear processes and documentation make it easier to monitor compliance requirements and identify potential risks.
- *Increased Employee Morale:* Employees' stress levels drop and positive engagement goes up when team members have clear direction and smoother processes.

As you can see, the right operational systems can be a major factor in a company's success.

The Mindset of Leadership

Most entrepreneurs and business owners have a vision for the companies they lead, including its products, services, target market, and more. However, those same leaders may overlook the details of how the business will operate.

As the leader, it's imperative to envision operational systems you can believe in, then put them in place as early as possible, and lead by example. (There's no better time than today to begin.) You must have the mindset which says, "These systems are important," and communicate that verbally, through written policies, and most importantly by your behavior. If you aren't willing to follow procedures, and are intentional about doing so yourself, others will not feel the need either.

In addition to leading the way, I recommend you empower at least one other team member to be an operational systems champion, taking ownership of the entire set of procedures. This will be the company's go-to person for all things operational. Large corporations have COOs. That's great, but you don't need a high-level executive championing your operations. An organized employee who loves the mission will be more than adequate. Your operational systems champion must understand the value of protocol and how all departments interact with each other to produce the right outcome for your customers. (I'll expand on this below.)

You will determine the level of authority given to this role, as you may want to be out of the day-to-day operations and just oversee results. Or you may not be ready to take your hands off and wish to continue as the final decision maker for a time.

Does Structure Limit Creativity?

When encouraging a business to implement operational systems, one common pushback is that structure limits creativity. This is completely false. In reality, structure reduces confusion by setting parameters, providing the perfect environment FOR creativity. Of course you want your team to be creative, but you need them to know where to apply that creativity. Systems provide a framework for maintaining balance between creativity and practicality, so the ideas generated are not just imaginative but also implementable.

Categories of Operational Systems

In the next chapters, we will explore various types of operational systems in detail. For now, here is a list of operational systems by category in alphabetical order, along with a few words of explanation:

- Accounting: Financial tracking and reporting.
- Communication: Facilitating internal and external dialogue.
- CRM: Customer relationship management and sales support.
- Customer Support: Managing customer inquiries and service requests.
- File Management: Storing, accessing, and sharing business documents.
- HRMS: Streamlining human resource tasks and employee management.
- Inventory Management: Efficient stock control and procurement.
- Marketing and Sales: Supporting customer outreach and sales processes.
- Project Management: Organizing and overseeing tasks and projects.
- Security and Data Backup: Protecting business data and maintaining continuity.

For each of these categories you will want to consider how you manage them, what tools you need, and how they interact with one another.

Connecting Operational Systems

Let's talk about my favorite part of operations ... connecting them. Operational systems cannot be created in departmental silos. Serious consideration must be given to how one department's systems interact with the systems of every other department which also performs a task connected to that system. This is a somewhat complex concept which I came to understand by experience.

During my career journey, I worked at a marketing agency in an executive administrative role. My job was to support the President, but somehow I got involved in how things flowed operationally. My workstation was located in the center of all the departments, and I couldn't help but engage when someone side stepped or altered a process without understanding the effect on the next person in the process.

Before long I became the hub of all business processes, and the trusted source for coworkers when they weren't sure about a procedure or wanted to change something. In fact, our Creative Director gave me a funny title and award one year at our Christmas Party which reflected this role.

I share this nostalgic moment to underscore the importance of creating cohesive systems. I made it a point to understand how I was affected by the person's work before me, and how my tasks affected the person after me. That helped me make improvements in operational systems for the entire team, while fulfilling the ultimate mission of excellent service to our clients and keeping the company profitable.

(Incidentally, I was quickly promoted to a leadership position in that agency, overseeing all operations, and I eventually became a partner.)

Summary – and Looking Ahead

I hope this chapter has given you a clear picture of operational systems as the nuts and bolts of business operations, plus the benefits of having organized operational systems which connect with one another across departments. We'll dive deeper in the next chapter as we build an example company and its operational systems which admittedly have room for improvement.

Chapter Two

A Sample Company's Operational Systems

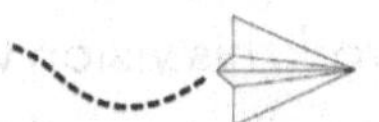

James Bean and JB Marketing

Let's look at a fictitious company to better understand the roles of each operational system and their best practices. The fictitious company is JB Marketing, owned by James Bean. JB Marketing is an agency which helps businesses market on the internet. The idea came to James when his friend, Sheila, shared plans to promote a product she created.

At the time Shiela approached James, he was managing a small retail boutique. His stated duties were to oversee employees and help wherever needed. However, the owners soon discovered he had a knack for the marketing aspects, such as product displays, store layout, and social media management.

Because the shop did not have an e-commerce platform for selling online, James approached the owners about creating a website. He even offered to learn the necessary skills on his own time if they would let him use his new knowledge to help Sheila as well, since her product did not compete with any items in the store. This was perfect for everyone. Win-win-win.

James immediately took a course in web development and discovered talents he never knew he had, learning technical platforms easily, and possessing a good eye for design and layout. Before long, he was able to create and launch his first two websites—one for the shop and one for Shiela. He found the work exhilarating and dreamt of doing this for other businesses. That is when JB Marketing was born, with the full permission and blessing of the retail shop owners who were benefitting greatly from James' skills.

He registered his LLC and began networking. Even though he loved doing the actual work, his vision was growing, and he knew he wouldn't be able to handle everything himself forever. James decided to be the Marketing Consultant for his clients and add freelancers to his team for graphic design, web development, and social media marketing.

JB Marketing's Current Situation

It is now one year later, and James is operating JB Marketing full time, with a team of independent contractors he regularly relies on. The retail shop where James previously worked is actually a client, at a reduced rate to show his appreciation for them helping launch his marketing career.

JB Marketing has other clients of course, in fact ten of them, and new leads come in mostly by word of mouth. James wants to grow JB Marketing by increasing the client base, offering new services, and transitioning to a team of W-2 employees instead of independent contractors. He's very excited about these possibilities.

Still, things are not too bad. Monthly gross revenues are over $25,000, with nearly $6,000 going to the bottom line. James won't be buying a yacht soon, but he's making a living.

JB Marketing's Operational Systems

On the following pages, we'll look at the operational systems introduced in Chapter 1, once again in alphabetical order, to see how JB Marketing functions currently in light of each.

- *Accounting:* James is using Microsoft Excel spreadsheets for financial reporting, and Microsoft Word Templates for creating client invoices. While this seems to work for now, there are several drawbacks. With no automation in place, the tasks are more time-consuming than they need to be. Limited financial reporting capabilities make it difficult to really understand what's going on with the numbers. And the processes are disconnected from one another, requiring multiple entries of the same information.

  James' CPA has encouraged JB Marketing to move to a QuickBooks subscription, a suggestion which he's considering and should likely implement soon.

- *Communication:* James uses Google Workspace tools—Email, Chat, and Meet—to communicate with his team internally. Client meetings take place in person or via Zoom. There are no visible gaps or pain points at present.

- *CRM (Customer Relationship Management):* JB Marketing's client contact information is stored in James' personal Google Contacts account, which is only visible to him. Spreadsheets are used to track descriptions and fees for recurring services, and customer emails are stored in Gmail folders. When a client sends a request via email, James forwards that to the appropriate team member.

These systems are far less than ideal for effective customer relationship management. Client information is not readily available to the team, there are no records of customer calls, and the processes do not allow integration between email and client records. With James as the middle man, his time is often required for tedious activities.

- *Customer Support:* James is the sole point of contact in the business, using his cell phone and email address for all client interactions. This obviously is limiting.
- *File Management:* Digital files are stored in a folder system within Google Drive, which is one element of James' personal Google account, while physical documents are kept in James' office. Any items which need to be shared are sent by James to his team via email.

  Because James is highly organized, he knows where every file is, but the burden of document retrieval always falls on him. What's more, each team member then stores the files the way they deem best. Their systems differ, without a common protocol. Sometimes things get lost, forcing James to duplicate work.

- *HRMS (Human Resources):* Although JB Marketing is officially an LLC, James operates it as a sole proprietor with contractor agreements across the team. Independent contractors, by definition, get to set their own schedules, so the company is dependent on their inconsistent availability. It can become a juggling act to meet customer timeline expectations.

- *Inventory Management:* JB Marketing does not sell products, so conventional operating systems around inventory management are unnecessary. Office supplies are kept in a cabinet and ordered when James notices they're running low. Any breakdown in this ad hoc method causes a panicked run to the store or excess shipping charges.
- *Marketing and Sales:* As a marketing agency, JB's website is excellent. James does the Search Engine Optimization (SEO) and social media posting himself. He enjoys these tasks, but they take time away from client service and networking. A monthly eblast featuring marketing tips is sent to clients by one of the independent contractors.

  These efforts create a trickle of inbound leads, but not nearly the volume needed in order for the business to grow as James would like. Instead, the company relies heavily on word of mouth for new business.
- *Project Management:* Projects are managed with a free version of a project management platform. Unfortunately, it has no CRM module, so there's no way to merge the project information with client data. This complimentary version restricts the use of key features which have the potential to streamline processes, and it allows only one user, which of course is James. He keeps track of all one-off projects, recurring services, and task requests to his team.
- *Security and Data Backup:* An outsourced IT firm manages all JB Marketing's IT needs. They provide monthly maintenance of his computer equipment and backup cloud storage of all data on his computer and

Google Drive for a flat monthly rate. James has access to additional IT support outside the monthly plan at an hourly rate as needed.

This area of James' operations is serving him fairly well, but there is a pain point. Since JB Marketing has only one internet service provider in place, any internet downtime becomes a nightmare.

There you have it. A complete rundown of operational systems within a small business. We'll revisit James Bean and JB Marketing toward the end of the book to see how these processes worked out as the company grew, and how they might have been revised and improved over time.

What's Next?

In the next five chapters, we will dive deeper into each category of operational systems introduced in Chapter 1. And for this exercise I have rearranged the list according to the order in which that exploration will occur. Each chapter will take on a group of these categories, defining what they are, how they impact a business, and best practices for making them most effective.

Chapter 3

- Accounting: Financial tracking and reporting.
- Inventory Management: Efficient stock control and procurement.

Chapter 4

- HRMS: Streamlining human resource tasks and employee management.

Chapter 5

- Marketing & Sales: Attracting and converting leads into customers through aligned systems.
- Customer Support Systems: Keeping customers happy and loyal through systems that improve communication, service, and long-term retention.

Chapter 6

- Project Management: Organizing and overseeing tasks and projects.
- File Management: Storing, accessing, and sharing business documents.
- Communication: Facilitating internal and external dialogue.

Chapter 7

- Data Security and Backup: Protecting business data and maintaining continuity.

We've come a long way, but there's still plenty of ground to cover in this world of operational systems and business operations.

Chapter Three

Accounting and Inventory Management Systems

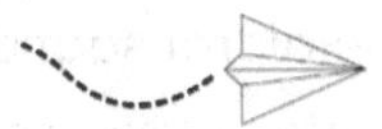

Know Your Numbers

Any seasoned business owner will tell you that knowing the numbers is critical to business success. It's imperative to be aware of how much income the company generates and from what sources, such as services, product sales, or both. Next is understanding how much of that income goes to each type of expense, and therefore how much profit the company makes. Equally important is being aware of the level of company resources tied up in inventory or supplies. Without knowing your financial and inventory numbers, you will be unable to make wise decisions.

Should the company take out a loan for expansion? Hire new employees? Buy additional equipment? Can the owners distribute a year-end bonus? Are tax payments up to date? Does the business carry the right product mix? Is there enough merchandise in stock to handle a seasonal surge in sales? Is everything in the warehouse saleable at full price, or should some items be discounted before they expire and have to be discarded at a total loss? And what about supplies like paper, toner, packing and shipping materials: are there enough available, or too many?

The operational systems of accounting and inventory management can help determine answers to these questions and more.

Accounting and Inventory Management Defined

Accounting involves everything to do with the financial side of a company. Accounting operational systems control the way a business records its financial transactions, then reports on those. By analyzing those reports, business owners can gauge the health of their companies and make adjustments for the future.

A company's inventory includes the physical items the business owns which it intends to sell to customers, and the supplies which the company will use itself. Inventory management operational systems govern which items the company will procure and in what quantities, and how the business will keep track of that inventory as items move in and out. These systems ensure that the right amount of inventory is available at the right time to meet customer demand without overstocking or understocking.

Accounting and Inventory Management Operational Systems ... Their Importance

We've already briefly discussed the importance of knowing your financial numbers and inventory. In this section we'll look at that more closely.

- *Report Creation:* The end result of all your accounting and inventory management operational systems will be the creation of financial reports filled with important information about your business. These will be discussed in detail later in this chapter.

- *Decision Making and Planning:* Business owners must make decisions about what's happening in the company today, and what's likely to be the case in the future. These are directly affected by how much profit the company is making, how much money is in the bank, any debt the company owes, and what the financial picture looks like down the road. Without clear data, the owner is flying blind. The right financial operating systems can help avert disaster and keep the company moving in a positive direction.
- *Transparency and Accountability to Stakeholders:* Operational systems which communicate financial information to partners, investors, and advisors are a must. These stakeholders want and need to know what's happening in the company, and finances are usually the most important part of that story.
- *Controls:* Companies which don't keep a close eye on their finances and inventory are vulnerable to errors, theft, and fraud. Suspicious activity will show up quickly when effective financial operational systems are in place.
- *Improved Cash Flow:* Systems which help avoid overstocks of supplies or saleable items reduce inventory carrying costs, which in turn has a positive effect on cash flow.
- *Customer Satisfaction:* On the other hand, out-of-stock conditions create frustration in customers who want to purchase the missing item. The proper inventory management systems can eliminate this problem.

- *Tax and Legal Compliance:* You do NOT want to get in trouble with the IRS or other government agency. They are unforgiving, and the penalties and interest add up quickly. Early in my career, I worked for a CPA (Certified Public Accountant) who specialized in helping people with tax issues. Those were tough cases and he had to really know the law in order to reduce tax liens or negotiate payment terms.

  Small business owners must manage tax obligations to avoid penalties and cash flow issues. These could include estimated quarterly taxes, payroll taxes (Social Security, Medicare, unemployment), and state sales tax. Businesses selling products or services in multiple states must navigate nexus laws which are especially critical for e-commerce. A professional may be helpful for maximizing deductions to reduce taxable income. For example, as of this writing there is a Section 179 deduction which allows full equipment cost write-offs in the purchase year, offering significant tax benefits. Your professional will know if this and other regulations change, are discontinued, or are replaced by newer programs.

  The key to avoiding costly mistakes is proactive tax planning. So consider working with a tax expert who does more than just file returns, but who strategizes year-round to minimize your tax burden and keep you compliant. With proper systems, nothing tax related will fall through the cracks. These are a must for every business owner's peace of mind.

Accounting and Inventory Management Operational Systems ... First Steps

In this section, we'll assume your company has no accounting or inventory management operational systems at all. What preliminary steps must you take to get them set up?

- *Consider a Mentor:* These first steps are so important that you may want to consider engaging someone to help, especially if this is your first business. Your mentor could be a business consultant or veteran business owner who can provide some real-world experience.

  I learned a great deal about accounting operations from previous supervisors and employers who became my mentors. I've implemented much of what they taught me into my own processes, such as how to handle payment terms in a new business agreement, ways to stay on top of paying bills to keep good credit with vendors, and more.

  I won't repeat this recommendation for every point in this section, although it certainly applies to them all and to just about every area of this book. But I will say it once again: Consider a mentor.

- *Select a CPA:* A Certified Public Accountant, CPA, is a licensed, accredited professional who can assist with many initial and ongoing financial matters. If your company is anything more than a minor hobby, you'll definitely need a CPA to help with tax filings if nothing else. You'll want a firm which is available for quick needs and willing to meet throughout the year if you wish, to discuss your business finances, challenges, growth plans, and other concerns. Ideally, your CPA should be familiar with your industry.

- *In House vs. Outsourced:* Will you be doing the functions of your accounting and inventory management operational systems yourself, hiring an employee for these tasks, outsourcing to a third-party provider, or some combination of these options?

- *Determine the Type of Your Business Entity:* Business entities include sole proprietorships, partnerships, Limited Liability Corporations (LLCs), S-Corporations, C-Corporations, and various non-profit organizations. There are pros and cons of each, including various tax ramifications, depending upon exactly what your business will do, the number of principals involved, expected revenues, growth plans and much more. Changing the entity type for an ongoing company can be complex, so give serious thought to this decision from the start.

- *Select Accounting Software:* Several options exist for accounting software, from a simple combination of Microsoft Word documents and Excel spreadsheets to highly sophisticated enterprise systems. My preference for small businesses is QuickBooks.

  At minimum, you'll want a system in which you can create customer invoices and sales receipts, enter and pay vendor bills, keep track of funds in and out, and generate basic reports from all entered transactions. Additional features which can be very helpful include the ability to link your system to your bank accounts in order to eliminate duplicate entries, automation of recurring transactions, inventory management, activity tracking so you can see a history of who did what within the system, customized reports, etc. Your industry may have other requirements or specific needs as well.

It's much easier to begin with the right software than to convert to something new a year or two down the road, so I suggest investing in a platform and systems which can grow with your business in terms of increased transaction volumes and complexity.

- *Open Business Bank Accounts:* Keeping your personal finances separate from your business finances is a must. Any personal start-up funds invested in your business will be entered as owner contributions in the accounting system.

  You'll need a business checking account to use for operating expenses and receiving customer payments. If you have W-2 employees, I recommend a separate checking account for payroll, in order to add a layer of confidentiality to these records, and also because payroll transactions can be complex due to the tax entries involved.

  As soon as possible open a business savings account. In fact, there's no better time than day one, even if you can only put a few dollars a month aside. These funds can be moved to your operating account if needed, but eventually you will build up essential cash reserves.

- *Secure a Business Credit Card:* Don't use your personal credit card for business purposes, or your company's financial records will become overly confusing. You will only need one business credit card unless you intend to provide them to employees. If you are unable to obtain an official business card, you can designate one of your personal credit cards for business purchases until an institution is willing to give your business credit. If you need to use a personal card for business, do not continue using it for personal purchases.

- *Implement a Chart of Accounts:* Your chart of accounts, called "Account List" in QuickBooks, is the backbone of your accounting structure. It shows every category of what your business owns (assets), what it owes (liabilities), the company's income (revenue), where it spends money (expenses), and its overall value to the owners (equity).

  Think carefully about the level of detail you want to capture as you record transactions. For example, will one revenue account called "Sales" be enough, or does your business need an account in the chart of accounts for each product or service category? Is one expense account called "Travel" enough, or do you want to list transportation, food, hotel, and parking costs separately? Your financial reports will be only as detailed as your chart of accounts.

  Some accounting software packages provide a default chart of accounts. New accounts can be added, and most can be revised or deleted, but others cannot, as they are mapped in the software to standard reporting such as sales tax filings, profit and loss, etc.

Accounting and Inventory Management Systems, Functions, and Best Practices

Each business is unique in the exact accounting and inventory operational systems it needs. Here are a few which I've found to be common, along with many of the specific functions and some best practices for each.

- *Bank Transaction Systems:* Every company needs a process for entering the financial transactions which run through their bank accounts.

  Study the features of your accounting software to see if there are automation options available. These could save significant amounts of time by linking your bank account to your account list, categorizing expenses automatically. QuickBooks does this, and other platforms may as well.

  Capture transactions in real time for the greatest accuracy. Weekly is sufficient for most small businesses. Larger corporations with a high number of transactions may choose to do this more often, perhaps even daily.

  Reconciling to bank statements should be done monthly as soon as the statements arrive. This is the function of cross-referencing what your accounting software says to what the bank statement says, and making sure everything matches, including the ending balance. If you have been auditing transactions throughout the month, this should be a simple process and also an opportunity to catch anything which may have been missed.

- *Financial Document Storage Systems:* Every financial transaction needs to be supported by a source document, such as a vendor bill, sales receipt, or copy of an invoice. A system will be needed for how the documents are stored. This will be a life saver in the event of a tax audit, warranty issue, and many other situations. Decide whether you want to keep them physically or if they will be scanned and stored digitally. We'll talk more about physical and digital document storage systems in Chapter 6.

- *Invoicing and Accounts Receivable (A/R) Systems:* These systems will determine how you bill customers and receive payments.

  Invoices and sales receipts should be detailed and clearly state what your customer purchased, be it a product, a service, or both. Vague invoicing or sales receipts create confusion and can increase the need for your customer to contact you unnecessarily. Will you be mailing an invoice or sending it via email? If payment is not collected immediately after a sale, send the invoice promptly, and be sure it shows your payment terms.

  Make it easy for customers to pay, with options such as a secure portal on your website for accepting credit cards in addition to taking checks by mail, but remember, there are fees associated with your credit card merchant. Having convenient ways for customers to pay will improve cash flow and reduce collection efforts which eat into profit margins.

  Your business deserves to be compensated for every transaction, so create an operational system for handling past due accounts. Review your A/R weekly, and send statements once a month, showing the client's outstanding invoices and their due dates. Communicate with predetermined letters, emails, and phone calls at set times, starting when invoices are past terms, then at intervals such as 30, 45, 60, or 90 days later depending on the needs of your business. Don't be timid or afraid to turn customers over to a collections attorney. And of course it is ok to extend grace for extenuating circumstances. Keep track of any totally uncollectable invoices and inform your tax professional of these at the end of the year.

- *Accounts Payable (A/P) Systems:* By paying your vendors on time and accurately, your company will establish excellent relationships with them and build a foundation for future credit opportunities if needed. With the right operational systems, none of their bills will get overlooked.
- *Internal Control Systems:* Operational systems around internal controls are critical if other people will be helping with your company's finances and inventory. These controls will reduce the risk of theft, fraud, and errors. Give serious thought to who will have access to what. This includes your bank accounts, warehouse or storage areas, supply cabinet, etc.

  Divide responsibilities in such a way that more than one person sees each transaction. This increases the chance of an error being caught or suspicious activity coming to light. Many companies require two signatures on all checks or those over a certain amount, and dual approvals on major transactions, especially wire transfers.

  If salespeople or account executives are allowed to invoice clients themselves, require that a supervisor sign off, ensuring invoice amounts are accurate, and eliminating the possibility of intentional or unintentional misrepresentation. This procedure could also be considered part of your billing system. (Sometimes operational systems overlap.)

For major purchases, require the owner's sign off, and at least three vendor proposals. If looking for a new insurance policy, for example, have the employee in charge or your assistant obtain three quotes with a comparison of the coverages and cost for each. This will help you make good decisions and avoid purchases you don't want. It's a good practice even if you are doing all the research for a purchase yourself.

Never use the same computer or software username and password for multiple people, especially for accounting applications. This allows the business owner to track user activity and prevent unauthorized changes. One of my clients suspected an employee was stealing when customers paid by cash. By viewing the audit portion of QuickBooks, I could see someone was changing the amount of cash sales, but since several employees used the same login information, there was no way to identify the culprit.

Designate one credit card for all general business expenses, recurring charges, and major purchases. If you must give credit cards to employees, be sure they have low spending limits and credit lines and provide them only to client-facing and administrative team members who need to make in-person purchases for the business. Have two people audit all credit card transactions no less than weekly.

- *Payroll Systems:* These operational systems are only necessary if your company has employees or pays yourself W-2 wages. If that is the case, there are a few items to consider.

Will you be using a payroll service or handling this in house? A payroll service understands tax and reporting requirements and will typically take care of all that for you, but of course they charge fees. Either way, whoever is in charge of your payroll systems should understand how to process taxes on both the employee and employer side and how they tie into your liabilities and government filings. Even if you're not processing payroll internally, this knowledge is valuable.

If your company offers benefits payable by payroll deduction, you will need a process for tracking and reporting them. These may even involve expenses on both the employee and employer side, so be aware.

How often will you pay employees and when does payroll need to be processed to meet the payday deadline? For example, if payday is every Friday, your systems must be such that funds hit employee bank accounts, in the case of direct deposit, or that paychecks are received from your payroll service or are written internally by Friday morning.

Be careful when classifying team members as hourly or salaried employees, as there are IRS regulations around these distinctions. In addition, it is important to understand the difference between an employee vs. an independent contractor and legal requirements for both. Employees fall under W-2 classification and are entitled to minimum wage, benefits, and tax withholdings while contractors are classified as 1099 workers responsible for their own benefits and taxes. If a business owner misclassifies employees as independent contractors, they could face fines, back taxes, and even lawsuits. Many businesses are in violation without realizing it, and the consequences can be devastating if there is a complaint. When in doubt, consult an employment law attorney.

Determine how commissions, bonuses, and salary increases will be handled. Have a way to track these and report them to all necessary parties.

- *Financial Planning Systems:* Before setting out on a road trip, it makes sense to have a map and know where you want to go. That's what an expense budget and revenue projections do for a business. They are detailed financial plans with goals for income, expenditures, profit, investments, etc. over a set period of time.

  You may have large cash needs each quarter or at the end of the year for items such as corporate taxes, bonuses, holiday gifts for clients, or a company event. These can be captured in your budget so the money will be there when needed. You can even create a special bank account or what's called an "envelope" in QuickBooks in which to set aside funds to have ready in the future.

  Budgets help eliminate unwanted surprises in spending. Rather than discovering all your computers are obsolete at the same time, requiring a significant cash outlay, you can plan to replace them one by one over a year or two.

  Having revenue projections gives your company a goal to shoot for. The goals should be reasonable, based on historical data and taking into consideration industry trends, as well as future marketing and sales efforts.

  If you do choose to incorporate these processes, consider delegating responsibility to key personnel to manage specific categories of it. For example, you could place someone in charge of creating team-building events, then establish an annual budget for that based on the company's team-building goals. Tell the person overseeing this initiative to track their spending against the budgeted amount and report to you regularly, making sure not to go over budget. Knowing there are spending limits can free you from feeling the need to be deeply involved. It will also create buy-in from the responsible person by helping him or her feel more empowered to execute the mission.

- *Operational Inventory Systems:* This type of inventory is made up of everything your business uses to operate, such as office furniture, computer and audio-visual equipment, phones, supplies, etc. Many of these items will be classified as assets in your accounting software, and it is important to keep track of them for insurance and tax purposes. This can be done in a simple Microsoft Excel spreadsheet, which should be updated periodically.

  You'll also want to keep track of supplies on hand, to avoid those frantic trips to a store or excess rush shipping charges.
- *Saleable Products Inventory Systems:* A business which sells products needs operational systems for receiving and selling merchandise. Some accounting software programs have automated features to help with this. Orders should be checked upon delivery if possible, certainly not more than 24 hours later. Contact vendors promptly if there are inaccuracies or damage.

These operational systems should include a process for monitoring stock levels to avoid shortages and surpluses, determining the optimal quantity and timing to replenish inventory, and procedures around who can place orders and how.

Include a recurring schedule for auditing your actual inventory against the numbers in your computer. This should be done no less than annually, with many companies conducting physical inventories every quarter. Regular spot checks will help catch any problems before they become major.

- *Inventory Storage Systems:* What are the storage needs of your inventory? Reduce space waste with proper shelving that is adjustable as needs change. Store your products in an orderly manner with proper labeling. Use the first in first out method by putting newer items behind items currently on your shelves, reducing the chances of products expiring or becoming outdated before you can sell them.

  Keep the storage area locked with access granted only to approved personnel. Install security cameras and use keypad locks in place of standard keys, so you can change the access codes easily when there is personnel turnover.

- *Inventory Forecasting Systems:* Develop systems to analyze sales volumes and any expected increases or decreases due to seasonality and/or upcoming marketing promotions. Use those projections to determine order quantities. If suppliers offer price breaks for higher volumes, consider taking advantage, assuming other considerations such as product shelf life and cash flow allow.

Financial Reports – The Heart of Accounting and Inventory Management Systems

A key purpose behind all the suggestions, functions, best practices and systems mentioned in this chapter is this: creating financial reports. Financial reports give management important information about the health of the company. There are many types of financial reports. Below are descriptions of several. Your particular business or industry may require others, and perhaps not need some of these.

- *Profit and Loss Report (P&L):* This report, sometimes called an "income statement," shows the financial performance of the company within a specified time frame. This includes revenues, expenses required for production of the company's offerings, and overhead expenses such as rent, utilities, and other ongoing costs. The report will contain as much detail as the chart of accounts allows.

  Based on all the data included in the P&L report, the bottom line will show a number. If sales are higher than expenses, the report will show a profit, indicated by a positive number. If sales are lower than expenses, a negative number indicating a loss will appear.

  An accounting software program such as QuickBooks has the capacity to run reports showing percentages of income by revenue type, percentages of expenses to revenue, year to year or month to month comparisons and much more. This information can provide valuable insights. For example, you'll be able to see trends, spot areas where you may be overspending, and find opportunities to increase profit margins from specific services or products.

The profit and loss report should be reviewed no less than monthly. It is one of two essential reports for any company. The second one is the balance sheet, described a little later in this section.

- *A Word About Accounting Methods:* There are two distinct accounting methods used in business. They are called "cash basis" and "accrual basis." Cash basis accounting tracks revenue transactions only when actual cash is received, and tracks expenses only when they are paid. Accrual basis accounting tracks income as it is invoiced, whether payment is received or not, and tracks expenses when they are incurred, whether the bill has been paid by the company yet or not.

  If you are running a small business or are a solopreneur, cash accounting is ideal. However, if you are planning to get investors or grow big, accrual accounting is most likely the better route to take. Many businesses run profit and loss reports on an accrual basis throughout the year, then file their income taxes using cash basis, with adjusting entries made to reconcile the books. Talk to your accounting professional to determine which one makes most sense for you, both for obtaining helpful business data, and from a tax standpoint.

- *Balance Sheet:* A company's balance sheet focuses on its financial position, providing a snapshot of three main financial areas on the date the report is run. Those areas are assets, liabilities, and shareholder's equity, sometimes called owner's equity.

Assets are anything the business owns, such as equipment, furniture, inventory, vehicles, money in the bank accounts, accounts receivable, etc. Liabilities are what the business owes, both short term such as vendor invoices and the current month's credit card balance, and long term such as bank loans and lines of credit. The balance sheet will break down these numbers in as much or as little detail as you wish. For example, inventory could be just one number, or you could split out the amount by individual products in stock. This would of course need to be set up in the chart of accounts.

The shareholder's equity number on the balance sheet is derived by subtracting total liabilities from total assets. This roughly determines the book value of the business.

Determining which purchases are assets rather than simple business expenses can be complex and dependent on IRS guidelines. In addition, certain assets depreciate over time, affecting their value on the balance sheet. Your tax professional will be able to advise in these areas.

It is recommended to review the balance sheet no less than monthly, looking for trends and paying special attention to critical resources such as cash and receivables. Shareholder's equity should be increasing over time. If not, changes need to be made somewhere in the business.

- *Cash Flow Report:* Having an idea of the funds which will be available at various points in the future can be helpful. This information is found in the cash flow report. Cash flow reports look at sales and payments the company is likely to receive, and bills coming due over a period of time, predicting cash levels along the way. This tells management when to curtail spending, and when it's safe to expand or invest.

Some businesses are seasonal and must build up cash reserves to sustain themselves during slower parts of the year. Others may need to look at the times of the month when clients pay versus when bills are due. If expenses hit on the first of the month, but clients are paying on the 15th, you may need to make adjustments.

- *Reports for Tax Purposes:* Businesses are subject to a myriad of taxes, depending on the type of business entity, products and/or services sold, location of the company, and other factors. Taxes can be due monthly, quarterly, or annually. Your tax professional will tell you what reports he or she needs to be certain your filings are accurate.
- *Quarterly Financial Reviews:* Create a system of quarterly reviews with your fiduciary advisor or CPA. Your financial professional will use these times to catch any errors, plus identify trends and areas for improvement by analyzing statements such as profit and loss reports, cash flow data, and balance sheets. This is also a great opportunity to assess estimated tax payments, so you won't be over paying or under paying, putting you at risk for penalties.

  These meetings are a great way to find money you didn't know you could save, spot deductions you missed, or uncover other ways to improve financially with the help of your CPA or other financial professionals. Structured processes help business owners stay in control of their financial future, reduce unexpected tax liabilities, and maximize profitability.

- *Financial Planning for Sustainability:* Regular strategic planning meetings can open your eyes to opportunities for building wealth and reducing financial risks. As wise King Solomon wrote so long ago in his book of Proverbs, chapter 21, verse 5, *"The plans of the diligent lead to profit as surely as haste leads to poverty."* *NIV*

  Endeavor to build a cash reserve fund to cover three to six months of operating expenses, as this will provide stability in uncertain times. Business owners should also establish retirement plans for themselves and their employees as soon as the company can afford it, as this will increase employee retention and long-term financial security. And it's never too early to think about an exit strategy—whether through eventually selling, transferring to family, or merging. Diligent planning today leads to positive outcomes in the future.

Accounting and Inventory Management Systems - Conclusion

You now know the definition of accounting and inventory management as they relate to business. You understand the importance of effective, well-thought-out operational systems for these areas. You've learned where to begin.

This chapter included a list of accounting and inventory management operational systems, their functions, and best practices. Your company may not need all of these, and might even require others, depending on your industry. And you've learned the purpose behind all these efforts: to create financial reports which will provide the information you, other stakeholders, and your tax professional need for anything related to the monetary and physical resources it takes to run a company.

It's been quite an undertaking, but well worth it as you continue on the path to business success.

Chapter Four

Human Resources Operational Systems

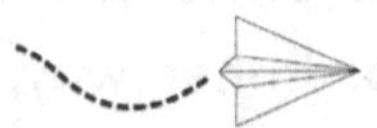

Human Resources: The Heart of a Business

Look around the location of any company. Desks, chairs, computers, supplies—even inventory—can all be obtained by anyone with available funds or credit. What makes one company stand out from others is its people. Attracting, retaining, and getting the most out of the best people largely depends on the Human Resources operational systems the company has in place.

Defining Human Resources (HR) and HR Systems

To understand what is meant by the phrase "human resources," often abbreviated as HR, let's break down the phrase. A business has resources. We often think of those as physical items, accounts receivable, and cash in the bank. But humans are also a resource, in fact a very important one. So human resources are just that—the people who are employed by a business.

HR systems, or Human Resources Management Systems (HRMS), therefore, are the series of processes and procedures a company creates to manage its team members. These systems begin at the first contact between the person and the business, continuing throughout the entire employment lifecycle.

The Importance of HR Operational Systems

Unlike other resources, humans have the capacity to manage themselves. However, there is no way any group of individuals would function in a consistent, effective manner without guidelines. In a large company, HR operational systems are handled by a dedicated HR department. Smaller firms and startups may rely on the owner him or herself or another key person for this purpose. Either way, the assigned person or department is responsible for all things personnel related and plays a vital role in the overall success and efficiency of an organization. Here are some key aspects of HR systems within a business.

- *Employee Experience:* Employees spend a large portion of their lives on the job. The degree to which they enjoy or dread that time will be affected by the systems they need to follow while there. A company with poorly defined, ambiguous ways of doing things will breed confusion, inconsistency, a lack of caring, and even unhealthy competition among the staff. While clear processes keep everyone moving in the same direction, toward desired outcomes.
- *Company Reputation:* People talk about the places where they work. You want them to say good things about your company. When a business is organized, the reports employees share with family and friends are much more likely to be positive. This applies even to those who eventually leave and go elsewhere. An effective set of HR operational systems will help make this a reality.
- *State and Federal Compliance:* There are laws for human resources to which every company must comply. For

example, specific forms must be completed by new hires within a certain time after their start date, then stored for a designated period after an employee's exit. Knowing what is required and having the proper systems in place will keep your company protected.

- *Defining the Employee Lifecycle:* Human resources operational systems outline the ways new talent is recruited, employees are onboarded, team members are supported throughout the duration of their employment with training and performance reviews, and how terminations are conducted if necessary. Without these systems defined clearly, the employee lifecycle would be chaotic.
- *Employee Data Management:* Information about employees will be used to determine eligibility for benefits, when to schedule performance reviews, qualifications for salary increases, available and upcoming personal time off, training needs, and post-employment requests such as verification of employment. Operational systems are necessary to keep track of the necessary data.
- *HR Communication Channels:* Team members need to know how to communicate regarding the human resource aspects of their employment. Where do they direct questions about payroll, company policies, benefits, basic company news, and more? What are the processes for doing so? Without defined systems employees will lack the ability to engage on these important matters.

HR Operational Systems ... First Steps

Whether you are adding employees to your business for the first time or have a staff already but no formal HR processes, use this list as your step-by-step guide for getting started.

- *In House vs. Outsourced:* Will you be tackling your company's HR functions yourself, outsourcing them to a third-party provider, utilizing an online solution, or going with some combination of these options? A variety of consultants, vendors, and digital platforms exist which provide HR services.
- *What About a PEO Company?:* PEO stands for Professional Employer Organization, also known as Employee Leasing or Staff Leasing. These firms provide comprehensive Human Resource services and can save time and money by streamlining HR operations, and simplifying compliance and risk management. This can be a great option for small businesses.

  When a business uses a Professional Employer Organization, the PEO and the client company (such as your business) co-employ the client company's staff. Taxes are filed under the PEO's Federal Employment Identification Number (FEIN), but the client company maintains full control over the employees. That control includes all decisions regarding hiring, firing, performance management, day-to-day operations, and anything else concerning the employee. The PEO is there to assist and offer guidance for any of their services, but the client company gets the final word.

  PEOs offer services around payroll, benefits administration, Worker's Compensation insurance, tax compliance, employee onboarding, leaves of absence, personal time off, unemployment claims, and more. Because a PEO pools all its clients together, they can offer a wide range of employee benefits at rates small businesses are often not able to offer on their own.

Here is a list of topics business owners should consider when thinking about whether or not to engage with a PEO:

HR and Administration: Is the owner struggling with payroll, benefits, compliance, or handbook updates?

Compliance and Risk: Does the company need help with employment laws, workers' comp, or unemployment claims?

Employee Benefits: Is there a need to offer better, more competitive benefits, which the owner finds too costly or complex?

Payroll and Taxes: Are those responsible for these areas overwhelmed by payroll processing, tax filings, or compliance?

Growth and Scalability: Is the business expanding or needing flexible HR solutions across multiple locations?

Cost and Efficiency: Would a PEO provide savings and stability in the company's HR-related expenses?

Strategic Focus: Are HR tasks distracting leadership from focusing on business growth?

Before hiring a PEO, confirm the company is certified by the IRS by checking the public listings on the IRS website. While having this certification is a signal the organization may be trustworthy, it is by no means the only way of indicating whether a PEO is right for your business. It's important to research and compare capabilities, as no two PEOs are exactly alike.

- *Become Familiar with Employment Laws:* Research all local, state, and government employment regulations pertaining to your industry and the size of your company. Be sure to include any locations where you have remote employees.
- *Clarify Your Companality® Vision:* Just as a person has a personality, a company has what a former business partner of mine called a Companality®. In fact, he registered a federal trademark on that word. A more generic term for this may be "organizational culture." As you think about any company with which you do business, you'll realize there are certain characteristics, attitudes, etc. which affect your experience with that business. This is its culture. (For more information, see the book, *Companality®: Developing Intentional Organizational Culture*, by Steve Fales, available on Amazon.)

  What characteristics do you want to define your organization's culture? Will it have a buttoned-down atmosphere like a high-level New York law office, a more laid back California surf shop vibe, or something in between? Are team members expected to grind it out all day, or is fun on the agenda? For example, some companies have training videos running in the break room, while others have a foosball table. There is no right or wrong, within industry parameters, but it's important for leadership to define the type of culture they want before developing HR operational systems.

- *Create an Organizational Chart:* This is a visual representation of your company's personnel structure, showing the various roles, how they relate to each other, and the chain of command. Every function or department will be represented, including human resources. We will go into more detail regarding organizational charts in Chapter 8.
- *Define Needs, Roles, and Objectives:* This step will require brainstorming as you create a list of every HR-related area in which you will need an operational system. Broadly speaking, one portion will cover employee recruitment, onboarding, development, retention, and exit. Another will capture all the roles you wish employees to fill now and in the future. Objectives which will require systems might include improving employee satisfaction or aligning new hires with overall business goals.
- *List Your Desired Policies:* Think about the elements you feel are important to the organization's culture. For example, will you include a code of conduct, dress code, strict attendance rules vs. flex time, etc.? What systems will you need to communicate and enforce those policies? Spend some time with this exercise.
- *Establish Your Company's Compensation and Benefits:* Determine a compensation range for each role within your organization. Which positions will be paid via salary, hourly, or commission? Be sure to understand the legalities of each. Consider benefits such as healthcare coverage, professional development training, personal time off, etc.
- *Create Essential HR Documentation:* Based on the decisions you made in the previous steps, it is now time

to create the actual job descriptions, new hire paperwork, employee handbook, and other documents to support your policies and procedures. Online resources may be a huge help in this step.

- *Set up Your HR Systems:* Write out the step-by-step processes needed to support all aspects of the human resources elements of your company. Utilize software and related tools as needed. The next section of this chapter will provide some tips for this.
- *Implement and Train:* The final elements of your initial steps are to implement the Human Resource operational systems you devise and train your team accordingly. This is not only one of your first steps, but will be an ongoing process throughout the existence of your business.

Human Resource Systems, Functions, and Best Practices

We have laid the foundation by explaining the importance of HR operational systems and created a list of necessary first steps. It's time to go into more detail regarding the functions of these systems and some best practices. The systems discussed will be divided in two parts: 1) Those implemented in a logical order through the recruiting and hiring process; and 2) Systems affecting all team members all the time.

As systems are developed, remember, every one of them is a representation of your company's workplace and will impact how team members feel about working there.

HR Systems Implemented During Recruiting and Hiring

- *Help Wanted Job Postings:* Job postings should contain more than the title, responsibilities and necessary qualifications for the open position. This is an opportunity to promote your culture by including a brief company overview and what it's like to work there. Use wording which is also included in the corresponding role description. (See the next bullet point.)

  Highlight aspects which will attract the kind of people who match the culture and are likely to eliminate those who don't fit. Phrases such as "We work in a fast-paced environment with a high volume of client requests" will deter people who prefer a slower pace and can't keep up with rapid workflows.

  Some qualifications will be required while others may be preferable but not mandatory. A college degree, for example, might be preferable but optional if the applicant has enough relevant work experience.

  Stating salary details may help screen people who are looking for a certain income. In my experience, when declaring a salary range, people assume they will receive the higher end. This can make it difficult to offer at the lower end if they are not qualified for the greater amount. So, include criteria to justify the points within the range. You can always offer more to a candidate during a later step. Highlight benefits, perks, and any compensation which is over and above the base salary.

- *Role Descriptions:* Create clear role descriptions for each position within the organization. Include the appropriate title, department or team for the position, chain of command, key responsibilities, and performance expectations. It's okay to state specific tasks but even better to describe areas the employee is expected to own. Instead of "answer phone calls and greet visitors," a better description could be "ensure all communications and interactions at the front desk are handled promptly, professionally, and in alignment with company values." Include wording which allows for growth or additional responsibilities as needed. Use bullet points for clean and easy reading. Much of this information can also be used in job postings. (See above.)

- *Assessment Tools:* This is a great way to screen candidates during the interview process. There are several types of assessments available for a variety of needs or reasons. For example, skills assessments evaluate a candidate's ability to perform tasks such as typing, data entry, accounting, using computer software, and more. Aptitude assessments look for reasoning capabilities such as numerical, verbal, logical, abstract, or situational judgment.

  Consider searching the internet, then using one or two for all candidates, plus additional assessments when applicable for specific skills needed within a role. Making these part of the interview process will also weed out candidates based on their level of interest. If someone is not willing to take an assessment, they are not motivated enough to work for your company.

- *Interviewing Candidates:* Outline a step-by-step process from job application through interview to final decision, including the what, when, and who. Your company's decision makers do not have to participate in every step of the interview process, but they will need to get involved eventually. Some applicants will be eliminated from the pool early on, while others will progress to the next step. Outline the criteria which will require input from decision makers and include them in at least one session with the candidate.

Prior to the first meeting provide details such as typical working attire, location address including floor and suite if applicable, parking tips, and a phone number in case they need to reschedule or get lost. Confirm receipt of all communication. The goal is to eliminate reasons for a failed interaction, while also setting the tone for the level of interaction expected within your culture.

Respond to all applicants even if they do not make it past the initial screening. This creates a positive impression of your company and provides closure. Not hearing back can be more frustrating than receiving an official rejection.

For those moving forward in the interview process, communicate next steps both verbally and written. The progression should be made clear, including the anticipated number of conversations, types of meetings (phone, in person, or video), who will be attending, and what future steps will be, including how and when they will be notified of your decisions.

- *Candidate Tracking:* Create a system for historical data on everyone who applies. It's not uncommon to see the same candidate more than once over the course of time, so having a history of whether they were interviewed or not, and if so, how it went will save time and avoid unnecessary repeat conversations or meetings. Include dates, interactions, impressions, previous documentation such as resumes, applications, etc., and names of internal personnel who participated in the process.

- *Making an Offer of Employment:* This is the final step in the interview process. When a candidate has successfully made it this far, you will need to prepare an offer packet, also known as a welcome packet, and determine how it will be presented. The packet should include an offer letter, a welcome letter from the CEO or President, documents which need to be signed such as non-compete agreements, a corporate culture piece, and anything else related to the offer.

  The offer letter should indicate the title the person will have, compensation, commission structure if applicable, start date, short explanations of benefits and time frame for eligibility, and next steps for accepting the offer. This is another opportunity to establish the level of professionalism in your culture.

- *New Hire Paperwork:* It can be beneficial to send all new hire paperwork before the first day of employment to give the employee time to review, ask questions, and complete the forms. This will also reduce the time spent with someone from your HR department on the person's first day, allowing more time to acclimate to the company culture and training schedule.

  Using digital forms with e-signatures, when possible, will streamline the process, reduce errors, and lessen the need for physical copies, although some forms such as the I-9 require the employer to see the employee's identification in person. Consider an online portal for new hires to access and store all required documentation in one place. Provide clear instructions and make yourself available for questions.

Your HR operational systems should include compliance measures on maintaining documentation as well as receiving it. Governments require some forms to be kept for a certain period even after an employee leaves the company.

- *Prior To Start Date:* Send a welcome message to the new hire prior to the start date. Include details of what to expect on the first day, such as start and end times, where to go upon arrival, who to ask for, lunch options, break times, dress code reminder, etc. Remind the new hire of anything he or she needs to bring: identification and completed forms for example.

  Make sure the workstation is properly and completely set up. Your pre-start date operational system should include a checklist of equipment and supply needs. This will reduce the time it takes to prepare. Test out all equipment and software, including printing, scanning, and telephone. Set up his or her email address and add the new hire to all internal resources such as employee directories, shared virtual spaces like Slack or Microsoft Teams, and anything else your company uses. This creates the feeling that the organization welcomes new employees.

- *Day One:* The best way to determine what to do on the first day of a new hire's employment is to put yourself in his or her shoes. Try to imagine what it would be like walking into a new position without any prior knowledge or experience working in your company. Then do everything you can to make it the most positive experience possible.

Having a greeting card signed by coworkers on the new hire's desk is a nice addition. If possible, schedule a team lunch. Collect all necessary new hire paperwork such as the W4 and I-9 forms, payroll processing information, and others which may be required by your location or industry. Develop organizational systems for walking new employees through HR platforms, making sure they know how to sign in. Go over company policies, procedures, and expectations allowing time for questions.

- *Onboarding:* This is an important part of the employee experience. Many studies show that a positive onboarding experience is correlated to long-term success for the new hire with the company. It involves familiarizing the new hire with key information about the company and the position, obtaining appropriate documentation, and introductions to colleagues. Don't leave the new hire alone to figure out what to do. Have a written schedule for the first couple weeks providing times for training and assignments.

  Incorporate as much team shadowing as possible. Split up the training among multiple current employees to reduce the number of interruptions per person and to give the new hire a variety of interactions and connections throughout the company. Include opportunities to shadow different departments so he or she can gain a bigger picture of the organization. This helps employees understand how their functions fit together, forming a greater sense of teamwork.

- *Initial Employment Period:* As of the writing of this chapter, there are no federal laws requiring an initial employment period for employees and most states do not have requirements. Unless your workforce is part of a union, employment in the U.S. is generally considered At Will, meaning either side can terminate the employment at their discretion within certain guidelines. Some states do make distinctions affecting unemployment compensation rates for employers regarding terminations during the initial employment period versus after it. Check with an HR professional in your area.

  Either way, it is best practice and commonly accepted that the first 90 days of employment is an initial employment period. This allows the employer and employee to evaluate each other. The employer is assessing the new hire's performance, and the employee is deciding if the company is a good fit. Whatever period you choose, communicate it during the interview process, document it in the offer letter, and recommunicate when onboarding.

  Conduct a check-in meeting at the halfway point of the initial employment period to not only communicate from the employer's perspective but to get feedback from the employee on their experience.

- *Assimilation*: Don't forget to create an operational system for acknowledging successful completion of the initial employment period to the employee and entire staff. This is another excellent opportunity to build a positive experience and reinforce your organizational culture.

Additional Human Resource Systems

The operational systems below affect all team members within an organization at every stage of their employment.

- *Mission Statement:* Why is your company in business? A response of, "To make money" may be satisfactory to owners and investors, but it probably won't motivate employees. Much better to have a stated organizational mission which can be communicated in a concise phrase.

  A technology company's mission may be, "To make communication among friends, family, and business associates easier." An air conditioning contractor might state, "To make our customers more comfortable." An insurance provider could have a vision of protecting the lifestyle of its policy holders, expressed in a few words which convey this message.

  Make the statement something easily memorized and repeatedly reinforced internally through visual representation, team meetings, employee documents, etc. Many companies share these statements externally in marketing materials, social media, and websites as well.

  Effective mission statements define what the business does, who it serves, and the value it provides. Ideally, they guide decision making and give the team a sense of purpose beyond just doing a job. And of course, when the statement is at the core of the organization's culture, the business really does make the world a better place.

- *Core Values:* These are the non-negotiables of your company culture. Defining them will help you not only communicate expectations to your team but also interview candidates with these values in mind. Take some time to identify what matters most to your business in terms of a team member's character and behavior.

For example, one of the core values in a previous company was "Make it easy for the customer." This affected everyone and everything we did. It put the focus on the other person and gave us an edge on the competition because we wanted to make sure anyone interacting with our company felt it was easy to do business with us. We not only applied this to our external customer but our co-workers too, who we called "internal customers."

What are your core values? Some examples to consider are honesty, integrity, always meeting deadlines, under-promise but over-deliver. Whatever you decide, make sure to incorporate them in all internal communications at every opportunity. Everyone, especially leadership, must know what the core values are, and behave accordingly.

- *Key Policies:* A company's leaders will need to decide which policies are critical enough to be included in their employee handbook, mentioned below. While this is also a first step, I've included it here as well because the key policies of an organization may change over time.

  Some standard policies include codes of conduct, dress code, personal time off such as vacations and sick days, leaves of absence, parental leave, performance reviews, disciplinary procedures, and much more. Consider when it's important to provide details and when it's acceptable to keep things general. For example, just saying "Casual Friday Attire" leaves this up for interpretation, so be more specific. An employee might think shorts, t-shirts, and flip flops are acceptable, while the business expectation was nice looking jeans, a collared top with sleeves, and shoes which are no more casual than clean sneakers.

Certain policies are required by law when a company hits a particular number of employees, is in a specific location or industry, or meets other unique criteria. It's best to check with an HR professional to make sure all bases are covered.

- *Employee Handbook:* Every company needs a comprehensive employee handbook which contains all company policies. Decide whether you wish to outsource the creation of the handbook to an HR professional or create it yourself. If tackling this internally, it's wise to have an HR professional who understands your location and industry review the handbook for legal compliance. Always include a signature page which states the handbook was provided, read, and understood by the employee. Have them also sign any new or revised policies.

  It is perfectly acceptable to provide your employee handbook to new hires upon acceptance of an offer, before the first day of employment.

- *Job Titles:* Job titles help clarify where each person fits within the organization, especially those with words such as "Manager," "Director," "Vice President," etc.

  Many titles are understood across all industries, others are industry specific, and some may be unique to your company internally. For the latter, consider adding a commonly used title as a subtitle during the recruiting process. For example: "Corporate Concierge (Administrative Assistant)". Corporate Concierge may fit your culture, but adding the term Administrative Assistant will make it easier for jobseekers to know what you mean.

- *Employee Data Management:* Employee information such as employment history, performance evaluations, salary details, contact information, emergency contacts, etc. should be maintained in a secure location. Paper documentation can be stored in a locked filing cabinet and digital copies in local or cloud-based folders, with access available only to HR personnel. Create an operational system for keeping these details up to date, including forms for employees to submit whenever anything changes, and an annual request for confirmation of the data you have on file. Do the yearly audit in December, to increase the likelihood of accuracy on W-2 forms, and confirm the information as part of the exit process whenever an employee leaves the company.
- *Employee Benefits:* Choosing the benefits to offer employees can be challenging. There are many factors such as cost, employees' needs and wants, recruiting leverage, flexibility, and availability. Don't just offer a benefit because it sounds like the right thing to do, make sure it makes sense to the business and staff.

  If you already have employees and will be offering benefits for the first time, conduct a survey to ascertain what is important to them. Currently businesses with fewer than 50 employees are not required to provide health benefits, but not providing this benefit limits the competitive edge when recruiting.

Consider benefits that are unique to your company. Some examples I've seen include reimbursement for continuing education up to a certain amount per year, additional paid time off around holidays, compensation for a certain amount of volunteer hours in the community, and cell phone reimbursement based on the expectation that employees will use their personal phone for business purposes. One company I know offered "Fun Money" for employees to use to do something they enjoy. The only requirement was to share their experience with the rest of the team during a staff meeting. Get creative but keep your costs in check and be sure that what you come up with is in line with your employees' interests.

- *Tracking Personal Time Off:* Personal time off, also known as PTO, can be paid or unpaid depending on your company's benefits package. Some companies make distinctions between types of PTO such as vacation versus sick time, while other businesses simply create one bucket for them all. Whatever you decide, you will need a way to track the amount of personal time off earned or accrued and used per employee. Your time off tracking system should also include procedures for requests, approvals, and keeping employees informed of PTO available.

  Let employees know how to submit requests for both planned and emergency situations. If an employee has a personal emergency or needs to call in sick, they need to know your preferred method of communication and who to contact. Some companies require an actual phone call while others allow text messages, some require notifying a direct supervisor only while others mandate informing the entire team as well. Decide what is best for your company so work is covered and no one who needs to know is left in the dark.

Planned time off requests may require advance notice, with a form to be completed and approved by a supervisor. A typical policy could be 30 days' minimum notice before requesting a week's vacation or two weeks' notice for taking a couple days off. The process will need to define who is responsible for making sure all the work will get done in the employee's absence and that all affected parties know what they need to do.

How will you determine if a time off request is approved? Considerations could include the PTO an employee has available, the company's needs, and/or seniority in the case of overlapping requests. In a previous company, it was determined that one executive needed to be on deck at all times, so leadership had to coordinate before scheduling time off.

The HR department or responsible party will need to track all requests to verify that employees have accrued enough time off to cover their absences, and to communicate this to the employee. This could be done in an online employee portal where updates are made automatically whenever the information changes. PEO platforms which handle payroll typically offer this service. If you are tracking manually, you will need a system of checks and balances.

Whatever you decide, an operational system around this key personnel benefit is extremely important. Your team will appreciate knowing the personal time off they have available and how to properly use it.

- *Training and Development:* A company's HR operational systems should include a training plan for each department and role. This could be a simple outline of the skills which require training and how that will be accomplished.

  A great deal of employee training will be done during the onboarding process, but it should not end there. Create opportunities for employees to continue developing in their roles through staying abreast of industry and technology updates, developing personally and professionally, and anything else which will increase their value to the company.

- *Performance Reviews:* Studies indicate that employees often become disengaged and ultimately leave companies when they do not receive regular or constructive feedback from their employers. Most employees expect a formal performance review annually. However, you don't have to wait until the first work anniversary to start the review process. Consider a review at the end of the initial employment period and another at the six-month mark. In fact, research indicates that casual reviews every 60 to 90 days are as important as the official annual review.

  Develop a clear operational system detailing all aspects of performance reviews including who will conduct them. This is typically the employee's direct supervisor. It is also wise to have someone in a human resources role attend to ensure the process is in line with company policies and to provide a neutral perspective.

  The most effective reviews involve a two-way conversation. Any forms should match the company's culture, and expectations of the employee's role. Give employees the form to fill out a week prior to the review, allowing them to complete it before you meet.

Performance reviews can also include peer feedback and/or leadership team input. Whatever you decide, make it consistent throughout the company and state the process in your employee handbook.

Keep in mind that employees often assume the annual review will include a salary increase, so be prepared for that part of the conversation.

- *Performance Monitoring:* In addition to formal reviews (see above), create a process for monitoring the performance of each employee and team on an ongoing basis. Include informal conversations during which staff and management can touch base briefly or have more in-depth communication outside formal reviews. The purpose is to gauge progress and offer mid-course advice as needed. Include a tracking system to capture the main points of these discussions, including any agreed-upon employee goals.
- *Career Path:* Companies offering advancement opportunities have an edge over their competition when it comes to recruiting and retaining top talent. This can be communicated through creating a defined career path. An advertising agency may have a career path for graphic designers, consisting of Graphic Artist, Graphic Designer, Senior Graphic Designer, Art Director, Creative Director, and Chief Creative Officer. Each position comes with a certain level of responsibility, salary, types of projects, and management opportunities.

Career paths must be outlined for each department in the company, even if there are only a few levels, such as Receptionist to Office Admin to Executive Assistant. These can be expanded as the business grows. Be sure your operational systems include the exact duties, responsibilities, and necessary skills for each role.

Let team members know how they can advance to the next level. Will that be based on time in a previous role, demonstrated capabilities, education, other criteria, or some combination? Consider whether or not you want there to be a trial period as employees move up, and if someone can move from one career path to another. For example, if your office admin expresses interest in sales, could he or she enter a new career path within your company?

- *Promotion from Within:* It is usually more cost effective to promote someone already working at the company than to train a completely new person. This also creates a positive culture, as employees see the business offering ways to move up. Before recruiting externally, share the open position internally as an opportunity for advancement. Look for people with relevant experience, interest in a new position within the organization, and potential for even greater responsibilities in the future.
- *Terminating an Employee:* Deciding to terminate an employee and going through with that decision is difficult for many business owners and supervisors. When it becomes necessary for any reason, whether a performance-oriented or behavioral issue, it is essential to have an operational system in place.

Meet with the employee and another leader or HR personnel to conduct the termination conversation away from other employees. Prepare in advance by familiarizing yourself with the team member's work history, performance reviews, and any other relevant information, so you will have clear, documented reasons at hand if necessary.

Have a termination letter ready, plus any forms for closing out benefits and providing necessary information to the employee. The letter should include an end date of employment, an explanation of accrued personal time off payouts, date of last paycheck, instructions for ending or extending benefits, procedures for returning company property, and a reminder of any non-compete agreement if applicable. Many states have strict rules about deducting the value of unreturned company property from an employee's final paycheck. I would advise against it.

When delivering the news to the employee, remain empathetic but firm. Don't make it about yourself with phrases such as, "This is so hard for me." I guarantee it is harder for the person being fired. Instead, simply state you are letting them go. Be careful not to say anything which would violate employment laws. Avoid blame or arguments by keeping the tone constructive and refusing to debate the reasons.

Give the employee a moment to process what is happening. Inform them of what they need to know, as mentioned above. Then tell them you will give them time to gather their personal belongings.

- *Exit Interview:* When an employee leaves a company voluntarily, I recommend an exit interview. This is an opportunity to share experiences and feedback which could help improve the workplace. Frame it as a learning opportunity for both sides. Questions to ask could be: "How was your overall experience working here?" "What did you enjoy most/least about your role?" "Do you have any suggestions for improving the company or management practices?" "Were there resources you felt were lacking?"

  Listen actively and stay neutral. Allow the employee to feely express thoughts without interruption or judgment. Acknowledge their feelings but avoid agreeing or disagreeing. Conclude on a positive note by expressing thanks for their contributions to the company. After the meeting, document the key points and any relevant feedback and look for trends which could be used to improve internal processes.

  Just as when an employee is terminated involuntarily, communicate next steps and details such as the last date of employment, an explanation of accrued personal time off payouts, date of last paycheck, instructions for ending or extending benefits, procedures for returning company property, and a reminder of any non-compete agreement if applicable.

HR Systems – Conclusion

You now have a solid understanding of the foundations of human resource operational systems, as well as the critical role corporate culture (Companality®) plays in shaping a successful organization. You've explored key concepts and best practices to help build and maintain a strong, cohesive team.

With this knowledge, you are better equipped to design HR systems which support your business goals and build a positive work environment.

As we continue our journey through business operational systems, it's time to turn our attention outward. Next, we'll dive into the areas of Marketing, Sales, and Customer Support—key functions which connect your organization to the market and drive growth.

Chapter Five

Marketing, Sales, and Customer Support Systems

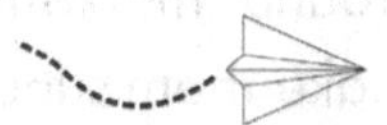

Attract Prospects, Convert Them to Customers, Keep Them Happy

The roles of marketing, sales, and customer support often get blurred, though they each have distinct purposes and require unique operational systems. Together, these areas of an organization create brand awareness, customer acquisition, and client retention.

Marketing's main purpose is to identify and attract potential customers, inform them of the benefits of doing business with a particular company, and drive demand for its products and services. Sales is the process of converting leads into customers through prospecting, pitching, negotiating, and closing deals. Customer support comes after the sale and is designed to answer questions, provide technical advice, resolve issues, and enhance satisfaction. These three functions are interconnected, and sometimes integrated, to provide a seamless experience throughout the customer lifecycle.

The Importance of Marketing, Sales, and Customer Support Systems

A company must generate revenue to survive. Having a great product or service will not be enough if the marketplace doesn't know it exists or if customers do not make regular purchases. And any market share gained initially must be maintained. Operational systems around marketing, sales, and customer support are needed to make them successful. Here are some key aspects of those systems.

- *Brand Identity, Awareness, and Demand through Marketing:* A strong brand can create loyalty, justify pricing, and differentiate a business from its competitors. Predetermined consistency in marketing efforts establishes a company's identity, reputation, and credibility. This is essential to help potential customers understand what the company offers, how it meets their needs, and why they should consider it over alternatives.
- *Converting Leads to Customers through Sales:* This is the most direct way for a company to generate revenue. A lead cannot turn into an income-producing sale if there are no systems in place to make that happen. Sales efforts can be executed by dedicated salespeople, or with an automated platform such as a properly set up e-commerce website. It is critical to have strong sales processes if a company hopes to grow or even survive.
- *Customer Satisfaction and Retention through Customer Support:* Providing excellent customer support encourages repeat business and increases the lifetime value of each customer. Relevant operational systems will provide the framework to resolve issues, answer

questions, and address concerns that lead to higher satisfaction levels.

- *Reputation Management through Customer Support:* A company's reputation is dependent on the quality of its interactions with customers. Delivering as advertised is only a first step. Exceeding customers' expectations will create better buzz about a business, and the right systems can turn negative experiences into positive ones. This leads to favorable reviews, testimonials, and word-of-mouth marketing.
- *Increased Revenue and Profitability through an Integrated Approach:* Marketing attracts potential customers, sales converts them to revenue generators, and customer support retains them for years to come. This integrated approach turns more leads into customers, keeps more customers loyal, and increases overall revenue and profitability.

Marketing, Sales, and Customer Support Systems ... First Steps

Use the list below to set up your systems if you are just getting started or as a reference to help you identify gaps in your current systems.

Marketing Systems

- *Determine Your Marketing Budget:* Every company, no matter what size, needs to invest in marketing. This mindset can be challenging for business owners who think they don't have the funds. There's nothing wrong with starting small. Over time, the budget can increase as the business grows and aspires to reach new levels. If you are unsure of a reasonable amount for your company's budget, consult with your CPA and/or a business mentor.

- *Consider Engaging a Marketing Professional:* It may be tempting to handle all marketing tasks yourself to reduce costs. This can be time-consuming, and result in wasted money on ineffective initiatives. Consider a marketing professional who specializes in small businesses and your specific industry. Research your options, ask people in your network for recommendations, and consider the pros and cons.

  If you choose to outsource, determine who inside your company is going to direct the outside agency's efforts, approve their recommendations, monitor results, and request adjustments if warranted. That person will need stated guidelines for his or her decisions.

- *Define Marketing Objectives:* What do you want your marketing to achieve? Broadly speaking, desired results can range from pure brand awareness, such as stating what makes your company unique, to solely lead generation through strong promotions. Most companies land on a mix of the two. Determine your firm's objectives, so you can be sure the operational systems and messaging will always be in line.

- *Identify the Target Audience:* Brainstorm ways to capture the profile of your ideal customer. Consider demographics such as age, gender, income, geographic location, and more. Other factors to think about are their interests, preferences, pain points, etc. If your business offers multiple products or services, you may have more than one target audience profile.

- *Choose Marketing Channels:* Channels are the methods and media which companies use to promote their brands, products, services, and any special offers. These include social media platforms, email marketing, search engines, television commercials, radio, direct mail, print publications and others. Ponder which of these are most likely to reach your target market, and invest your marketing budget accordingly.
- *Develop a Content Strategy:* Determine the types of content to be utilized for your business. This includes colors, graphics, illustrations, messaging, offers, etc. Create a calendar showing which messages and/or offers will be placed when and where, and what the costs will be. Update this calendar with actual information after the content has run, including notes about each effort's effectiveness.
- *Select Marketing Tools:* Some marketing channels can be managed using automation tools. This is especially true for digital forms of marketing such as email and social media. Do some research to determine if there are tools available to streamline the time it takes to execute your marketing plan.
- *Track Marketing's Effectiveness:* Because marketing is a significant expense in most companies, it's important to know which initiatives are the most effective. Develop a system to help leadership determine if the company is gaining greater exposure among its target market, and the right types of leads are being generated. This information will help guide future decisions.

Sales Systems

- *Define the Sales Process:* Outline the flow of sales efforts, including lead generation, qualification, nurturing, closing, and follow up. Decide who will perform the actual selling of your company's product or service. Will this be your own responsibility, the task of salespeople, or will you rely on a digital platform such as an e-commerce site? Determine how each step in the process will be implemented.
- *Select a Customer Relationship Management (CRM) Tool:* A CRM is used to store information on a company's contacts, track interactions with them, and automate common sales workflows. There are many CRMs available, some of which are quite robust, though also complex. Research to select the one you feel is best, considering how it will integrate with your other marketing systems.
- *Develop Sales Scripts and Collateral:* Create scripts for verbal communication, templates for written transactions, presentations for more structured opportunities, and printed materials to support your team in various stages of the sales process. If your sales funnel utilizes automation, be sure to pay attention to these elements also, as they can become "out of sight, out of mind" if not careful.
- *Determine Sales Commissions:* Decide if a portion or all of your sales team's compensation will be via commissions. If so, create processes for how they will be earned, tracked, and paid. A typical consideration is whether to calculate commissions based on billings or collections. There are pros and cons. Consult an

experienced mentor or business professional if you need advice.

- *Setup Sales Key Performance Indicators (KPIs) and Metrics:* How will you determine whether your team's sales methods are successful? The answers are your Key Performance Indicators (KPIs), or metrics. KPIs measuring sales efforts could be the number of phone calls or sales meetings during a week or month. Sales results could be measured by conversion rates from prospect to paying customer, dollar amounts of average sales, sales cycle lengths, etc. Use tools to monitor these metrics and provide reports for review by leadership.
- *Train Your Team:* Prepare your team through initial and ongoing training using all the operational systems developed to this point and beyond.

Customer Support Systems

- *Define Support Channels:* These channels are how your customers will contact your company for support. Choose the methods you plan to use, such as phone, email, live chat, etc. The more options you provide, the better, to show clients you want to make it easy for them to get through to someone who can meet their needs.
- *Select Customer Support Tools:* Select software for your desired support channels. These tools should make it easy to view customer feedback, track interactions, and run reports. Leadership can then analyze the data to gauge effectiveness of the company's customer support.
- *Create a Knowledge Base:* Frequently asked questions (FAQs), tutorials, and guides are great tools for customer support. Create directives for their creation, a place to

store them, and ways for customers to access these assets.

- *Implement and Train:* Once the customer support tools you selected are set up, train your team how to best use them. Training must be ongoing to maintain a reputation of excellence for your company. A plan to make this happen is a must.

Marketing, Sales, and Customer Support Systems, Functions, and Best Practices

We have stated the importance of operational systems in the areas of marketing, sales, and customer support, and outlined initial steps for creating them. We will now go into more detail regarding their functions and best practices.

- *Invest Wisely:* Before committing to a significant marketing campaign, conduct tests on a small scale. For example, if you suspect your target audience spends significant time on social media, begin with organic posts. If you see an interest, and increased followers, move on to paid ads or boosted posts. Create a written plan and review it monthly or quarterly to track progress and return on investment.

- *Lead Generation through Networking:* A great way to market a business, and sometimes generate sales, is networking with other professionals. Have a strategy for finding groups which meet your company's goals, and for making connections within them.

  The best definition of networking I have ever heard came from the leader of one such group. He says, "Networking is not selling to each other but selling through each other." Another of his pearls of advice is, "Promote unto others as you would have them promote unto you."

When speaking with contacts, don't make it all about you. Instead, develop a list of questions for getting to know other members, then look for ways to help them through referrals. Decide how you will learn what is working for their companies and apply those practices to your business. Define any special offers and discounts for those in your networking groups.

Make networking a consistent part of your business development plan by committing to a set schedule for whomever will be participating in networking groups. Implement a way to track connections and the ROI resulting from these efforts. This will help you determine an appropriate budget for future plans.

- *Brand Awareness through Consistency:* Building a recognizable brand requires consistency over time. The look, feel, and messaging must be uniform in every one of the company's marketing elements.

  Begin by creating a set of brand guidelines which includes your logo usage, color palette, typography, tone of voice, authorized imagery, and brand values. Require all marketing professionals and team members to follow the guide. Designate a centralized place with shared access to all marketing assets along with your Standard Operating Procedure (SOP) for developing content. Monitor regularly to maintain absolute compliance. This is essential.

  Think of building brand awareness as the long game. The pay-off isn't immediate but there is one if you stay with it. Eventually the marketplace will identify your company as soon as they see or hear anything your business puts out. Prospects and customers will immediately know who you are, what you do, and what separates you from competition. None of this will happen, however, without intentional planning, so spend time brainstorming the ways you will expose your brand to the public.

- *Marketing Plan:* Map out your marketing initiatives for the next twelve months. The plan should include channels you intend to use, offers, and messaging, all within a stated budget. This will become your blueprint, helping you organize and prioritize efforts. Whether simple or detailed, a pre-determined marketing roadmap provides a clear overview of past and upcoming activities, helping you stay aligned with your goals. By planning ahead and tracking results along the way, you'll execute campaigns more effectively and gain valuable insights to revise strategies and guide future decisions.
- *Leverage Digital Marketing:* There are many options for marketing a business online. Here are a few ways a company can make the most of its digital presence. Keep in mind that clear operational systems will be needed for each.

  Social Media: Learn the purpose of each platform, then select the one(s) which most directly target your desired audience. Begin by connecting through simple engagements rather than blatantly trying to sell. People are on social media mostly for personal interactions. Any offers you do make must flow from a natural conversation.

Share helpful information, interesting articles, fun facts, and the like. Occasionally post a unique offer or link to a specific page on your website with something readers will find beneficial. Many social media platforms also offer paid advertising opportunities. These postings can be more sales oriented.

Utilize a platform which seamlessly integrates with multiple social media sites, offering automation to efficiently create and schedule posts in advance. Establish a consistent schedule of crafting content, monitoring engagement, and evaluating performance to maximize effectiveness.

Search Engine Optimization (SEO): Having a beautifully designed website is not enough to attract customers. You will need to drive traffic there. One technique for that is called Search Engine Optimization, or SEO.

While there are many tactics to performing SEO on your site, one key element is identifying keywords and phrases for which members of your online target audience are searching. This can be done by using research tools such as SEMrush or Google Keyword Planner. Search engines consider specific wording and images to determine which sites are displayed highest in search results. Google's algorithm is complex and changes unpredictably. For example, as mentioned above, keywords are needed, but if they are overused the site will be penalized. Sound content strategy is required to gain high rankings, so a dedicated professional may be a worthwhile investment.

Search Engine Marketing (SEM): While SEO (see above) focuses organic efforts primarily on your site without direct payment, SEM utilizes efforts off your site which include both paid and organic strategies to gain visibility in search results. Paid efforts falling into the SEM category include search engine ads, also known as Pay Per Click (PPC), shopping ads, retargeting ads, paid social media, display advertising, video, affiliate programs, influencer marketing, and more. Each of these require budgeting decisions in addition to content and audience strategy.

Google My Business: If your business has a local presence, it is essential to set up a Google My Business listing. People use those to find a company's address, phone number, website, hours, and to read reviews. Make sure the information is accurate. Include photos for the best reflection of your company.

While only the verified owner or designated manager(s) have full control over your listing, Google does allow practically anyone to suggest changes. Sometimes those changes are accepted by Google. You will want your operational system to include a schedule for carefully monitoring your listing periodically to make sure no unauthorized revisions were made.

Online Business Reviews: Customer reviews are a major factor affecting a company's reputation. Consumers rely heavily on them when making purchase decisions. Reviews show up on Google My Business, Facebook, Yelp, and industry-specific platforms.

After providing your product or service, ask customers for a review and make it easy by sending a link to the appropriate page. This will increase the chances of building your volume of reviews, and the more the better.

What's more, if any negative comments do show up on your page, the effects will be diminished by a large number of positive reviews.

Responding to Online Reviews, Both Positive and Negative: It is best practice to respond to all reviews, good and bad. A "thank you" in reply to complimentary reviews adds a personal touch and another layer of connection.

Still, no matter how excellent your product or service, you will not be able to avoid negative customer experiences 100% of the time. If your customer support doesn't resolve the issue the situation may end up in a review. Responding tactfully is crucial to recovering from the potential damage a negative review could cause.

In order to respond, you will have to know a review is there. This requires monitoring all online review platforms. Software is available to automate the process or you can create calendar reminders for doing this manually.

Don't delay. Reply as soon as possible, certainly no later than three days. Work on diffusing the situation with an empathetic tone acknowledging the customer's concerns. Include the reviewer's name if possible, and mention something specific from their review. Offer a solution, and an apology if necessary.

Thank the reviewer for their feedback and take the conversation offline by providing a way for the person to contact someone who can help directly. Finally, highlight your business' strengths and how you are working to improve the customer experience.

Consumers understand that not all bad reviews should be given weight. How a company handles negative comments often has more impact on the brand's reputation than the review itself.

- *Email Marketing:* Email messages are another way to stay connected to your target audience. Consider the following when using this marketing method, then create operational systems for all your email marketing efforts.

  Become Familiar with the CAN-SPAM Act: Federal guidelines, called the CAN-SPAM Act, govern the sending of email by businesses. Complying is simple, although many companies are in violation without realizing it, exposing themselves to potential penalties. An internet search will return all the information you need.

  Utilize an Email Marketing Platform: There are several platforms providing email marketing services. It is advisable to use one rather than sending large numbers of emails through your email program. Most email providers have sending limitations. If you exceed the limitation, your marketing email could be marked as SPAM and your account may be suspended.

  Email marketing services, on the other hand, are allowed to send huge numbers of emails. Delivery percentages are typically higher than you could obtain from your own program, there are greater personalization options, and detailed analytics and reporting tools are available. It is therefore advisable to use one of these services.

  Use a Legitimate Email List: Build your own list of recipients who have done business with you in the past and/or have given you permission to send them emails. Be cautious about using purchased lists, as no one likes to receive unsolicited commercial email. This will help you avoid complaints which could lead to infractions related to sending SPAM.

Sender Email Address: Use a personalized email address as the sender rather than a generic email address such as info@yourdomain. Generic addresses are more likely to get flagged as SPAM on the recipient's end.

Write Compelling Subject Lines: The subject line is the first thing your recipient sees. Make it strong, compelling, and applicable to the content.

The most effective subject lines are those which give relevant information or make a promise. For example, a software automation company might say, "Our Clients Save An Average Of 57 Minutes A Day. Here's How." A brick and mortar shoe store could write, "The Most Comfortable Sandals You'll Ever Wear Are On Sale This Week Only." Put yourself in the reader's place and ask, "What would make me open this email?"

- *Responding to Customer Complaints:* Just as responding to online reviews is important (see above), an operational system for handling complaints which come to the company directly is equally critical. Here are some items to include.

  Always acknowledge the customer's concern by stating back to them what you heard. Use an empathetic tone whether in writing, in person, or over the phone. For example, "I'm so sorry to hear you didn't receive your order by the expected delivery date. We understand how important it is to get your items on time." Include how you will resolve the situation.

Complaints arriving via email must be addressed promptly. Determine the maximum time you will allow before someone replies, and state that as a policy. If your customer support person doesn't have an answer right then, he or she should request permission to get back to the customer later and be sure to follow up as promised.

- *Define Your Sales Process:* When it comes to a sales process, clear terminology is important. For example, what is the difference between a "lead" and a "prospect?" A lead is often a person or company you are trying to nurture, whereas a prospect may have already expressed interest in your service or product.

  Spell out what will happen at each stage of the sales process and how efforts will be tracked. Leads may be added to a campaign which automatically sends emails on a pre-determined schedule such as every two weeks. Prospects require greater attention, such as a personal phone call within 48 hours.

  When the opportunity arises to make an actual sales presentation, an additional operational system will kick in. This typically consists of the approach, setting expectations, overcoming objections, asking for the order, and making the final purchasing procedure smooth for the customer.

- *Preparing for a Sales Call:* Develop procedures your sales team can use to learn about their prospects prior to a sales call. Provide tips for doing research to gain understanding of the potential customer's history, industry, and competition.

- *Building Relationships throughout the Sales Cycle:* Strong relationships bridge the gap between what a company offers and consumers who need it. Teach salespeople to ask questions, listen, and reflect back during the conversation, and to tailor the presentation of products and services to the prospect's needs.

  It's easy to neglect staying in touch with leads, prospects, and even customers. So have a process which calls for consistent contact, and offer value with each engagement. Your system should stress the importance of transparent, honest, clear communication about your company's offerings, and require the staff to always do what they say they will. This will build strong relationships, creating valuable customers for years to come.

- *Saying "No" to a Prospect:* Not all prospects are a good fit for every business. It is better to walk away from a sale than to take on a customer outside a company's scope of expertise, resulting in headaches, lost productive time, complaints, a damaged reputation, and more. Give your sales team clear criteria regarding how to identify potentially incompatible prospects early in the sales process, and explaining how to move on in a professional manner.

  Always maintain a respectful tone. Express gratitude for the prospect's interest, communicate your inability to fulfill their need with a brief explanation, and offer an alternative if possible.

- *Focus on Value-Based Selling:* Sell solutions, not products. Prepare a comprehensive list of the unique benefits specific to the product or service your company offers. Explain how each benefit will solve your customers' problems and provide a return on investment.

  Your sales team must become completely familiar with this list, ready to refer to it from memory during sales presentations, so include training sessions within the process. As prospects see the value of your offerings, they will be much more apt to buy.

- *Adding Even More Value:* An effective way to cement customer connections is by providing free resources showcasing your expertise. Offer eBooks, webinars, guides, or consultations. Programs which reward existing customers who refer your business to their network of friends, family, and colleagues can also be a value-add.

- *Develop an Effective Proposal Process:* An effective system for sales proposals begins with templates for each of your company's offerings, and guidelines for exactly how the sales team will use them. This will streamline the proposal process and maintain control over what prospects are told.

  Include areas where custom information can be inserted to personalize the document. It's especially powerful to reiterate what was learned during a prior conversation about the customer's current situation to show that your sales team is listening and cares rather than just trying to close a deal.

  Be sure the proposal template is clear on pricing, deliverables, and any customer efforts required to complete the project. For example, a marketing agency might outline what they will do when building a website and what they will need from the client such as photos, executive's bios, etc. Include a detailed scope of the project or physical items, payment terms, collection procedures, engagement length, termination options, and more. You may even wish to have an attorney review your proposal templates to make sure all bases are covered.

- *Presenting Proposals:* A proposal is usually created after an initial meeting with a prospect. Determine how proposals will be presented. Will salespeople send the proposal attached to an email, or must they make an in-person presentation? In cases where the prospect is geographically distant, a video meeting can be a good option.

  Most companies find it best to avoid blindly sending proposals with the hope that the prospect will respond. Just because you had a great first conversation doesn't guarantee they will receive your proposal with the same enthusiasm you have when sending it.

  Either way, be sure the team is clear on how your company wants proposals to be presented, by having an operational system which spells out the necessary steps.

- *Training and Support:* The most effective marketing, sales, and customer support teams are those which receive ongoing training and strong backing from their companies. So, consider providing classes and seminars on a pre-defined schedule, along with a procedure for escalating customer situations if the need arises.

Keep in mind the culture you wish to create. Some companies use an aggressive approach and want sales reps to act accordingly. Others adopt a no-pressure consultative methodology. Customer support personnel might be taught to bend over backward to meet any client demands, or to hold a firm line on strict company policies.

- *Incentives:* Your systems can also contain rewards for highly effective marketing efforts, sales targets achieved, or customer support resulting in favorable reviews. The incentives could be either individual or team based, consisting of additional compensation, time off, or other large or small recognitions. Find out what motivates your people and customize accordingly.
- *Adapt and Learn Continuously:* The best insights regarding your company's marketing, sales, and support will come from customers and even people who inquired about your product or service but did not make a purchase. Asking for feedback is hugely valuable. The process should include a way to review what is said, possibly adjusting company procedures in response.

  Stay up to date on industry trends and best practices by assigning one or more team members to keep on top of relevant websites, organizations, etc. and report their findings to senior management.
- *Build a Customer-Centric Culture:* Customer service is not only for the support team, it is everyone's responsibility. Create programs to foster a culture where the entire staff, from front of the house to back of the house focuses on the customer. Consider every

interaction: phone conversations, voice messages, emails, personal contacts, and more.

Include instructions to use the customer's name in verbal and written communication. Capture information about your clients' preferences, needs, and previous interactions in a shared platform (such as a CRM, discussed previously) so the information is available to everyone who interacts with that customer.

Discourage complaining or negative talk about customers or clients, and reward team members who consistently display a customer-first mindset. This will encourage employees to follow these systems.

- *Be Prompt with Responses:* Quick response times are critical, whether the customer has a complaint (as mentioned earlier), a positive comment, or a simple inquiry. Delays erode the perceptions customers have about how sincerely a business values its customers. Outline acceptable time parameters for your company's replies in a clear operational system.
- *Be Proactive:* Will your company be following up with customers after providing a service or selling a product? If so, a stated policy will be necessary to make sure it happens properly. This can provide an opportunity to discover any issues or dissatisfaction, allowing you to offer a solution before the customer submits a formal complaint. If the customer is happy with the transaction, a follow up "thank you" will further enhance the relationship, often leading to repeat business.

Marketing, Sales, and Customer Support Systems - Conclusion

The purpose of this chapter was to provide a good understanding of the outward facing areas of a business: marketing, sales, and customer support. We discussed the unique role each plays within a prosperous organization, their key concepts and best practices, and operational systems necessary for keeping them effective.

As we continue our journey, it's time to turn our attention to fulfillment by looking at Project Management, File Storage, and Communication Systems—key functions which drive the execution of all business operations.

Project Management, File Storage, and Communication Systems

The Power Trio: Project Management, File Storage, and Communication

Every business and department within a business has projects to manage, physical and digital resources to store, and the need to communicate. Operational systems in these three areas are essential for the company to run efficiently.

Projects have a beginning and ending date, usually with several steps to accomplish in between. All this activity requires oversight. The right operational systems ensure that initiatives stay on track, achieving desired outcomes within the time allotted.

File Storage systems are needed to organize data and documents in such a way that everything is secure, and information is easily accessible when needed.

The ability for a company to successfully exchange information both internally and externally is made possible by well-designed communication systems. As a result, all team members, vendors, and customers have the information they need and misunderstandings are avoided.

When these three systems are in place and synchronized, they create a foundation for smooth workflows, efficient teamwork, and timely delivery of products and services.

Project Management, File Storage, and Communication Systems ... First Steps

As with any operational system discussed in this book, it is best to think long range. Envision your company as you see it in the future, in terms of the amount of data and documents likely to be generated, and the information which will need to be shared with all relevant parties. Then set up systems with that vision in mind. This will prepare the company for growth.

<u>Project Management Systems</u>

- *Define Purpose and Scope:* Outline the elements you want your project management system to track, such as deadlines, tasks, individual efforts, collaborations, etc. Consider the number of ongoing projects you may need to track simultaneously. Think about each person who will be using these operational systems and the ways they are likely to interact with them.

- *Choose a Project Management Tool:* Research project management tools and choose the one which best fits your needs. Ideally, it should also allow for expansion as the company grows.

- *Create Workflows:* Identify the steps required to complete the projects handled by your project management systems. Organize them into phases, with manageable tasks, milestones, assigned responsibilities, and deadlines. Include a process for prioritizing.

- *Structure Communication Channels:* Incorporate ways within the system for team members to provide updates on projects.
- *Configure Project Tracking and Reporting:* Establish systems to track and report project metrics based on the company's needs.

File Storage Systems

- *Decide What Needs to be Stored:* Most companies wish to maintain customer, employee, and vendor data, plus order histories, archives of past projects, marketing assets, financial data, and more. Legal, government, and IRS requirements must also be kept in mind.
- *Consider the Types of Storage Needed:* Will the company be storing files digitally, physically, or both?
- *Select a Storage Solution:* Determine where and how each file type will be stored. For example, digital files could be kept in the cloud, on a local server, on an external drive, etc. Physical files might be placed in locked cabinets somewhere in the office, or off site in a separate facility.
- *Create Organized Structures:* Outline consistent naming conventions for individual documents or data, the files which contain them, the folders holding the files, etc. This applies to physical storage within cabinets, and digital storage as well.
- *Establish Access Permissions:* Decide who will have permissions for each area of file storage, how you will provide access, and how you will maintain security

throughout the life of the business as team members come and go.

- *Develop a Backup and Retention Policy:* Determine how you will protect stored files from getting lost or destroyed, and how long each category of files will be retained. Consult legal, government, and IRS guidelines.

Communication Systems

- *Assess the Company's Communication Needs:* Determine who on your team needs to communicate with whom, internally between team members, and externally with customers and vendors.
- *Choose Communication Channels:* Consider the methods to be used for each area of communication. Common tools include phone, text, email, chat, video, and shared spaces. Look for tools which can be integrated with other systems for maximum efficiency.
- *Establish Communication Protocols:* Create guidelines for using each communication channel. Define response expectations and protocols across the board.

Project Management, File Storage, and Communication Systems Best Practices

We have outlined the operational systems of project management, file storage, and communication, and discussed first steps for setting them up. We'll now get into more detail regarding best practices.

- *Choosing a Project Management Tool:* Create a list of needs and wants. If you don't know where to start, research common functions of project management tools, then categorize them into two sections: Must-Haves and Wishes. Must-Haves are the critical features you cannot compromise. Wishes are features which would enhance the experience but are not critical to achieving the company's goals.

I once worked with a staffing company that had to move from one platform to another because they needed a CRM (Customer Relationship Manager) with a pipeline feature. The top Must-Have was the ability to perform a Boolean search across all data within an employee candidate's personal information—not just the most recent resume uploaded. Such a feature was not common among staffing agency platforms at that time. This top Must-Have helped us rule out unsuitable options. There was no point in migrating to new software if it didn't meet this critical need.

Don't rely solely on a platform's website to assess features. Instead, reach out to software providers with your list of Must-Haves to confirm their capabilities. For instance, during the staffing agency search mentioned above, the winning platform was nearly overlooked because this differentiator was not mentioned on their website. Upon contacting the company, we learned that the feature had recently been added, and a demo confirmed it was exactly what was needed. This saved time and led to the right choice after exploring other options.

Research and compare at least three tools. Take advantage of free trials and set up test projects to evaluate usability. If you are working with a platform representative, request what's known as a sandbox environment to test run the software. Always perform a side-by-side comparison of critical features and costs.

Be mindful not to get stuck in "paralysis by analysis," as it's likely no tool will meet 100% of your needs. Workarounds can often be found for missing features, but avoid too much of this, as efficiency will suffer.

- *Build with Your Future Team in Mind:* Even if you are currently filling every role yourself, build with a future team in mind. Plan each facet of a project, thinking of who will be responsible for completing tasks, tracking progress, and reporting.

  If your business does have employees, welcome their input as systems are being developed. The goal is to help each person accomplish their part with ease and efficiency. People at all levels of an organization often have excellent ideas to streamline operations.

  No matter the size of your company now, people who are not on board today will eventually be utilizing your systems. Imagine them stepping into the process. Will it be easy to understand how to do their part in managing projects, storing and accessing data, and communicating at all levels?

Project Management Basics

Don't overcomplicate your project management processes, but make sure you cover all the basics. The following tips will help.

- *Project Scope:* Before creating a project's structure and milestones, etc., define and document a clear objective so everyone understands what the project does and does not entail. Share this with those involved in the project, and store the document in printed or digital form in a place where it can be reviewed regularly as a reminder.

- *Break it Down:* Divide the project into manageable tasks with deadlines and milestones representing key stages of progress for each. Examples of stages could include Planning, Implementation, Documentation, and Close-Out. Within each stage would be specific tasks. This approach helps the team stay focused on overall progress while understanding where the project stands at any given time.
- *Build a Realistic Timeline:* Outline your milestones and deadlines before starting. Include all tasks for each milestone, factoring in turnaround times from each contributor. Bake in buffer periods for unexpected delays and awaiting client responses.
- *Collaborate with Your Team:* Identify all contributors to the project and clarify expectations. Assign responsibilities and encourage everyone to ask questions or raise concerns early in the planning process. Follow the RACI Matrix, which stands for Responsible (who's doing what), Accountable (who's on the hook), Consulted (who needs to be asked), Informed (who just needs updates).
- *Project Templates:* Templates are predetermined structures of milestones, tasks, and deadlines, providing a guide for managing projects within the system. Utilizing templates will significantly improve efficiency, especially reducing the time it takes to get things started. Identify recurring projects and create templates for each.

- *Monitor Progress and Manage Risks:* Track progress regularly through reviews no less than weekly, and a dashboard for visual support. Be proactive in identifying roadblocks to resolve them quickly. Identify potential risks and prepare contingency plans for the ones most likely to occur. Encourage the team to flag issues early.
- *Document Everything:* Create protocols for when and what to document, along with operational systems for doing so. Capture every interaction with clients and vendors, progress from contributors, key decisions, and meeting notes. Store drafts, revisions, final versions, and approvals of deliverables.
- *Keep it Simple:* Focus on the project's essentials: milestones, tasks, deadlines, and communication. (We'll discuss more about communication, below.) Don't overcomplicate your project management process with unnecessary data or overly technical tools if they don't help productivity.
- *Review and Learn:* Upon completion of a project, review how it went and look for opportunities to improve the system. Document lessons learned and use any takeaways to tweak the process for the future. The goal is to continually improve the company's project management operational system.
- *Integration vs. Consolidation:* Integrating a project management system with other tools can sometimes streamline processes. However, consolidating all relevant functions into one platform is optimal. For example, if the option exists to either integrate stand-alone time tracking software into your project management system

or use the one provided by the system itself, it is usually best to use the one included within the system.

- *QuickBooks Integrations:* One exception to the point above is integrating the project management system with QuickBooks. Many systems state they integrate with QuickBooks, however the results are not always seamless, potentially disrupting a company's financial processes. Should issues arise, you must rely on the project management software company to troubleshoot them, and those companies may be limited in understanding the structure of QuickBooks or financial transactions.

  There are two key things to understand when considering an integration with QuickBooks. First, how does the project management system map invoice line items to your products and services within QuickBooks and tie them to income accounts? Find out how much control there is over this mapping and determine if it will be in line with your reporting needs.

  Second, how is the information synchronized? Integrations follow either a one-way or two-way sync which refers to the direction(s) in which information is pushed. In a one-way sync, information goes only from the software to QuickBooks. In a two-way sync, information goes in both directions. This is critical to understand. If information comes solely from the project management system to QuickBooks, changes you make in QuickBooks will not be reflected back to the system.

  Be sure to understand how synchronization happens. Not all integrations are automatic, some require a manual push. Determine the level of control you have over deleted data. I have observed a loss of financial data due to a one-way sync integration. Anytime the project manager decided to delete an invoice in the project management system, it would disappear from QuickBooks.

- *Time Tracking:* Even if your business does not invoice by billable hours, tracking the time it takes to complete tasks is beneficial, especially for service-based businesses. Understanding how much time you and your team spend serving a client provides crucial insight into efficiency and value. If you find tasks are taking longer than expected, it may signal the need to evaluate and improve your processes. Alternatively, it could highlight an opportunity to renegotiate fees to better align with the value you're delivering and the results your time produces. Consider software which allows team members to easily start a timer or make manual entries as they work on projects or respond to client needs.

<u>File Storage Basics</u>

- *Organize Digital Files into Folders:* Organizing digital files into a folder structure will save time and reduce stress. Start by creating folders with broad categories based on major themes such as Clients, Projects, Financial Reports, etc. Break each category down into subfolders representing specific tasks, clients, or years. Avoid creating too many sublevels by limiting them to two or three layers when possible.
- *Digital File Naming:* Adopt clear, consistent naming conventions for digital files and folders to allow easy identification of their contents without opening them. Include key details for client-related files such as the client's name or abbreviation, brief description of the

content, and the date. For internal files tied to specific departments, use the department name instead of a client's name. Including identifiers for multiple versions of a document (e.g., v1, v2). Ensure consistency: client names or abbreviations used identically across all documents, dates in the same format, uniform sequence of information, etc. Create an operational process and enforce compliance to maintain organization and clarity.

- *Archive Outdated Files:* Create a standard protocol for when a file is considered outdated, and a system for archiving those outdated files. Have a main folder for Inactive or Archived Clients and move outdated files there when the client is no longer active with your company. Do this regularly to reduce clutter in your active file storage spaces and to maintain historical data in the event you need to revisit the information. Consider using cloud storage if archiving becomes too large.
- *Organize Routinely:* Establish a routine, such as a weekly cleanup, to maintain order within your file organization operational system.

<u>Communication Basics</u>

- *Establish Communication Expectations:* Determine who, when, and what should be communicated. It is better to overcommunicate than to assume everything is clear or someone else is on top of the situation. Don't rely on one method of communication, but use a combination of channels.
- *Define Clear Communication Protocols:* Select communication tools and methods thoughtfully, considering both delivery and response times. Aim to

streamline by using only one platform per communication method. If several software platforms in your business offer instant messaging, choose the one which best meets your needs and disregard similar features in the others. Using multiple tools for the same purpose can lead to confusion and make it difficult for everyone to keep track of conversations. Consolidating channels will improve clarity, enhance efficiency, and keep communication organized.

- *Email Communication:* This method is best for formal and detailed communication. Use clear subject lines which reflect the email's content. When replying, stay focused on the original topic to maintain clarity and organization. If a new subject needs to be addressed, start a new thread or locate the appropriate existing one. To enhance tracking and effective follow-up, consider tools which confirm when your email was delivered, opened, or read. These can enable you to tailor a follow-up approach if a response isn't received within the expected time. Following these practices within an operational system will maintain clear, professional communication and improve correspondence management.
- *Organizing Emails:* Develop a standardized system for organizing email programs to create consistency across the company. Create folders based on categories or subjects to help reduce inbox clutter. The inbox itself should contain only messages requiring attention. Once a message has been handled, it should be moved to the appropriate folder. Sent emails should also be organized in folders. Leverage the email provider's automation features whenever possible. Delete emails only when

certain they will not be needed in the future, but do empty your deleted email folder regularly. These processes will preserve important correspondence while maintaining a clean and efficient email system.

- *Instant Messaging:* Use instant messaging exclusively for communication which does not require tracking or documentation. Establish clear guidelines for the urgency level associated with this method. Decide whether instant messages demand faster responses than email, or if the two communication methods can be viewed similarly. If your company culture defines instant messaging as an urgent communication tool requiring immediate attention, be sure everyone understands that. Require that the instant messaging tool remains active during work hours and train employees to monitor incoming messages promptly. Additionally, provide guidelines for indicating when someone is away from their desk so others are aware messages may not be seen right away. These systems create clarity and consistency in how instant messaging is used throughout the organization.
- *Out of Office Communication:* Establish a standardized process for communicating extended time out of the office during business hours. Define guidelines for what qualifies as "extended time" and outline where and how these messages should be relayed. Create a consistent out-of-office message template indicating the duration of the absence and contact information for someone who can assist during that time. This can have a friendly tone, if that fits your company's culture.

Require employees to set an email autoresponder to notify senders of their absence and temporarily update their voicemail greeting with the same information, including the date and time when they will be back to work. Be sure everyone disables these messages promptly upon their return unless the system allows for automatic scheduling. This proactive approach fosters transparency, trust with clients, and smooth operations during team absences.

- *To Meet or Not to Meet:* While meetings are important, too many can disrupt productivity and hinder people from getting work done. To strike the right balance, organize meetings around recurring essential touch points. Evaluate the current cadence of meetings and consider consolidating some into one meeting weekly, bi-weekly, or even monthly.

  For example, a President of a marketing agency needed to collaborate frequently with his Executive Assistant. However, their constant interruptions back and forth made it difficult to stay focused. They devised a system to have a weekly touch base meeting. Anything which didn't need to be addressed immediately was saved for the weekly meeting. This reduced the number of interruptions and created a smoother workflow.

  Common regular meetings are staff meetings, department leader meetings, team meetings, and project meetings. Determine what is essential to your business, define the meeting purpose and agenda template for each one, and create a recurring event on the calendar.

For day-to-day communication, leverage the tools and systems in place. If something requires a meeting, first consider whether it fits into an existing recurring meeting. If not, only then schedule a separate session. The goal is to be intentional and strategic, so meetings add value and help the team stay focused on their objectives, minimizing unnecessary disruptions.

- *Meetings, Meetings, and More Meetings:* Verbal and face-to-face communication remains an essential part of effective collaboration. Meetings can take place in person, virtually, or over the phone, so establish clear guidelines for when to use each method. Before every meeting, define its purpose and prepare an agenda to share with participants in advance whenever possible. Stick to the agenda during the meeting and allocate time for participants to raise additional relevant topics.

  Assign someone to take notes, and place them in the designated digital system. Recording meetings can also be beneficial, but use discretion and comply with all applicable laws and regulations regarding consent. After every meeting, send a concise recap of outcomes and action items to all attendees to clarify alignment on next steps and maintain clear communication. These guidelines will keep meetings productive, focused, and well-documented.

- *Communicating Instructions:* Effective communication around instructions requires a combination of clear written explanations and well-structured steps. Break steps down into manageable actions and present them in a logical order so they are easy to follow. To enhance understanding, supplement written instructions with visuals such as screenshots, images, or annotated diagrams to illustrate key points.

Consider creating video demonstrations using tools such as Loom which can show tasks being performed on a computer or mobile device. Videos provide a dynamic way to walk users through steps, offering clarity that text and static images alone may not achieve. Combining detailed instructions with appropriate visuals can keep the message clear, actionable, and accessible to a wide audience. This minimizes confusion and helps recipients complete tasks accurately and efficiently.

Project Management, File Storage, and Communication Systems - Conclusion

We've built a solid foundation for the Power Trio systems—project management, file storage, and communication—and how they work together to support a company's production. We then explored key concepts and best practices to establish systems to directly enhance operations. With this knowledge, you are better equipped to run your business effectively.

Data Security Operational Systems

Securing Your Business Data

Think of all the ways you protect your home. Are entry points kept locked or unlocked? Do you have systems, such as security cameras or a sign saying, "Beware Guard Dog"? Who has a key? What are you trying to protect and why? And how vigilant are the efforts? As you answer these questions, consider this: your company's data security should be approached with the same level of care.

Technology gives business owners many options, promising to make their lives easier by automating tasks for efficiency. However, with these advancements come vulnerabilities to online predators trying to steal or damage company data. While we can't protect ourselves with 100% certainty, we can do everything within our power to cover all the bases. This chapter will help guide you through some key processes.

Data Security Defined

The term "data" refers to information which can be shared, transmitted, or processed. "Data security" is keeping your information safe from hackers, accidents, and anyone who shouldn't have access to your data files. Data security falls under the larger umbrella of risk management, a common business term which means just what it says: managing levels of risk to reduce the chances of negative outcomes.

The Importance of Data Security Operational Systems

Here are some ways data security impacts your business, and why every company needs systems around this critical operational aspect.

- *Protection Against Data Breaches:* A data breach is when someone or something obtains access to a company's data without permission. This damages the company's reputation, and can result in many different types of financial losses.

  A well-known password manager platform I use experienced a data breach some time ago. They did the right thing by sending a notice to their customers explaining what happened and assuring us that the hacker was not able to obtain any sensitive information, due to the encryption on their end. Nevertheless, I took measures by changing all logins I had stored. However, even though I am personally confident there is no longer any danger, it's been a challenge to make clients feel safe with this platform, and some have asked me to find an alternative.

  With the right operational systems in place, a company can guard against data breaches and the negative consequences which come with them.

- *Reduced Downtime:* When you rely on technology, there is always the risk of a break or glitch, resulting in downtime. Productivity comes to a halt, as employees are unable to get online to use software requiring internet access, or to access data stored only online. Operational systems are needed as backup plans to resolve these problems quickly or avoid them altogether. Otherwise, you could face not only unproductive team activity, but also lost revenue, missed communication from potential customers, and expensive fixes.

- *State and Federal Compliance:* Several laws exist concerning data protection and security. We'll explore this topic later in the chapter. For now, just know that data security operational systems are important to keep your company compliant with the law. You do not want to take risks in this area.
- *Data-Driven Decision Making:* A benefit to properly managing data is the ability to use it for decision-making. There have been many times I needed historical data to determine pros and cons for a business initiative. When data was stored and protected properly, I was able to create reports to aid the process. When no data was available, the decisions had to made based on guesses.

Data Security Operational Systems ... First Steps

In this section, I'll assume you have not yet intentionally considered data security for your company. What steps should you take to be confident your information is secure?

- *Consider a Mentor:* As mentioned in a previous chapter, having a mentor is beneficial for every area of business. Relative to data security, the right person would be a consultant or veteran business owner who can give you some real-world experience on appropriate measures.

- *Engage an IT Professional:* When it comes to data, you may find yourself swimming in a sea of technological jargon. This can create confusion, cause gaps in your systems, or lead you to make unnecessary purchases. An IT professional can be a huge help.

  Find an individual or company that understands the type of protection you need and let them guide you through the process of obtaining the right equipment, and utilizing it properly for data security purposes.

- *Know the Specific Requirements of Your Industry:* Nearly all companies need data security systems to some degree, but some industries and types of businesses have stronger requirements. For example, storage of customer credit information must be compliant with the Payment Card Industry Data Security Standards (PCI-DSS). Businesses with access to people's medical information are subject to the Health Insurance Portability and Accountability Act (HIPAA.) The General Data Protection Regulation (GDPR) has complex requirements, especially for companies in or serving the UK.

- Research your specific industry to give yourself a thorough knowledge of the obligations regarding data security, then create operational systems accordingly. Consult a legal professional if necessary.

- *Identify and Assess Risks:* Know the types of data you collect and how you will store that information. Understand the levels of confidentiality needed, vulnerabilities to potential threats, and consequences of a breach.

- *Designate the Players:* Decide who will have visibility to your company's data, then grant only the minimum level of access necessary for each employee to perform his or her duties.
- *Develop a Data Security Policy:* Before you can create actual data security operational systems, you'll need to hammer out the big picture of how data should be handled, stored, and shared within your organization. This will form the foundation of all related processes.
- *Implement and Train:* Your final first steps are to implement the plan you have outlined and train your personnel. The IT professional you selected may be valuable here. I will provide some specifics, with more detail, in the next section.

Data Security Operational Systems, Functions, and Best Practices

Now that you understand the importance of data security, we are ready to introduce a few specific operational systems, along with their functions and best practices. Some of these may not apply to your company, or you may need additional systems. Portions of this discussion will be somewhat technical, perhaps requiring the assistance of an IT professional for certain implementations.

- *Strong Access Controls through MFA:* Require everyone in the company to implement Multi-Factor Authentication (MFA) when possible. This is where a user must enter a code sent either by text, email or phone call in addition to a username and password when he or she logs into certain applications.

Allow team members to use their personal contact information for MFA tied to their own logins. Maintain the security of this process by having a main Admin login separate from other users, which is associated only with a company-owned cell phone kept in the possession of a supervisor. The Admin will have the ability to add, change, or delete individual employee access to the application.

- *Data Encryption:* Encryption converts data into unrecognizable code which is only readable once it is unencrypted by another computer program. You will often see this when you enter credit card numbers on a merchant's website. Once the full card number is stored, only the last four digits are visible, while the rest of the numbers are encrypted.

  Use data encryption when storing sensitive digital files on servers, in databases, and devices or when in transit. Humans will not be able to read any information even if they gain access to it. You may need to engage an IT professional to set this up.

- *Data Backup Operational Systems:* Make a list of all the data in your company, and where it is stored. Include network servers, desktop computers, laptop computers, wireless devices, and hard copies in file cabinets and boxes. Create operational systems for regularly scheduled backups of digital data to a secure location such as cloud storage or offsite servers. Hard copies of paper records can be scanned and backed up along with other digital data. This will enable recovery of lost data in the event of technology crashes or simple user errors.

Automating backups will ensure they are not forgotten, and doing them frequently based on how often your data changes will capture the most recent versions of your information. At minimum, backup your data weekly, though in some cases, even daily is not often enough.

Periodically test your backups by restoring portions of the data, to confirm everything is working properly, before you have a real incident.

- *Software Updates and System Patches:* From cell phones to network computers, we are all familiar with software updates and patches. Updates often encompass significant improvements and changes to an application. They can involve large downloads, and complex installation processes, while patches are usually smaller and quicker to install because they only address specific issues, which are often security vulnerabilities. By scheduling these when it's convenient, you will avoid the downtime which occurs when updates and patches are forced and begin installing automatically.

  Create operational systems to regularly check for and install software updates and patches for all applications used in your company. Talk to an IT professional if there is any uncertainty.

- *Firewalls and Anti-Malware:* Firewalls protect your internal files and networks from external threats by monitoring traffic and applying defined security rules to either allow or block traffic. Anti-malware programs scan software and files to identify and remove specific malicious code such as viruses, worms, and trojans from websites, emails, and downloads. These essential applications can even offer real-time protection by scanning files as they are downloaded, opened, or executed.

- *Disaster Recovery Plan:* Create disaster recovery operational systems to follow in the event of a breach or loss of data. The plan should include an inventory of hardware, software, digital and physical files, and a process for restoring all critical programs and information which was previously backed up.

  Have necessary software installed, or at least available to install on replacement equipment. Include a clear prioritization list. Regularly test your systems by conducting exercises to simulate different scenarios.

- *Keeping Physical Items Secure:* Store your physical computer, servers, and any currently unused devices in a locked, secure space with access only by select personnel.

  Develop operational systems to monitor access to these areas. If an item such as a laptop needs to be removed for use outside the secured location, document its exit and return with signatures. File cabinets containing sensitive data should be treated in the same manner.

  Have systems in place which require employees to log out of software and computers during times away from their workstations. If computers and other portable equipment are left in the office after hours, secure them to their desks.

- *Data Minimization:* Keeping unnecessary data clutters your digital and physical environments, makes it difficult to retrieve relevant information, and causes inefficient use of storage resources. An operational system should be in place which includes regular audits and the secure removal of unnecessary or obsolete data.

- *Third-Party Risk Management:* When engaging a third-party vendor, be sure to vet their security practices to understand how they handle data you share with them. Incorporate confidentiality clauses and compliance requirements in official agreements, and state what they are allowed to do with the information you provide. An attorney can draft language for this to protect your company from claims against your vendors.

- *Employee Training:* Your operational systems should include initial and ongoing live training for your staff regarding data security policies and best practices. Cover all risks associated with non-compliance, as well as their negative impacts. Teach your staff how to create strong passwords and recognize the ever-changing phishing attempts, scams, and other cyber threats. Training should be ongoing with regular updates about new threats and security measures. Require confirmation of successful completion for any instruction provided.

  This education is also an unofficial company benefit, as it will be helpful to employees on a personal level.

- *Data Storage Audits:* Conduct routine audits of employees' computers to be certain they are following protocol in how data is stored. When team members save files to folders on their own work computers rather than on a network server, that data could be lost unless each computer is backed up regularly.

- *Incident Response Plan:* Create a clear incident response operational system to quickly react to and mitigate security incidents. Outline processes for both employees and management. To whom should an employee report anything suspicious or real and what method should they use? This could be a simple email to a person who oversees your IT needs, or a more elaborate procedure such as a designated form. Include steps for management to prioritize these reports and respond appropriately.

- *Intrusion Detection and Prevention System (IDPS):* An IDPS is software which monitors a computer system for threats and takes action to stop them when identified, eliminating attacks which may otherwise have slipped through. Depending on the specific setup, an IDPS can automatically alert administrators, launch banishments, change security environments, or modify the assault on your data. This security system has the benefit of enforcing policies continuously without human involvement, limiting the number of employees who interact with sensitive information.

  Obviously, an IDPS is a highly sophisticated application. Consult with an IT professional to determine if one could benefit your business.

- *Managing Passwords:* Use a secure password manager software for storing and sharing company or employee logins. Do NOT use Microsoft Excel files or Word documents or any other unsecure method for storing your logins.

  If you must provide login information to someone other than through the password manager, share it only verbally, or send the username and password in separate communications. For example, you might email the username, then send a text message with the password. Update all passwords frequently. Having an operational system around managing passwords will keep your company much more efficient and secure.

- *Creating Strong Passwords:* Provide a standard guide for creating passwords. Longer passwords with a mix of upper and lowercase letters, numbers, and special characters are best. Your operational system should instruct employees to use a unique password for each account and avoid personal information such as their birthdate, name, or phone number. One idea is to use a string of random words which is both long and memorable. Avoid common substitutions like "@" for "a" or "3" for "e". Avoid keyboard patterns such as "qwerty" or "123456". For optimal protection, use a password generator from your password manager platform.
- *Company Accounts:* Use a general company email address such as Admin@[your domain], Operations@[your domain], or General@[your domain] for all company owned online accounts and applications. Avoid using an employee email address, as this increases the chance of losing access to an account should the employee leave the company. Use employee email addresses exclusively for software logins unique to individuals, and be sure to have Administrator access tied to the general company email address, with authorization to add, change, or delete all employee user accounts and logins.
- *Communication Strategy:* Develop an operational system to inform customers, regulators, stakeholders, and other affected parties of any data breaches or breaks. The system should include the what, who, and how you will

communicate. Include the necessary details and steps the recipient should take, but avoid verbiage which might cause unnecessary alarm.

- *Legal Compliance Audits:* As mentioned earlier in this chapter, there are local and federal laws around data security. Develop an operational system to monitor your processes regularly and to check for new regulations to maintain compliance. Consult a legal professional if necessary.

Data Security Systems – Conclusion

You now know what data security is, what it includes, and how it interacts with your business. You understand the importance of securing your business by having operational systems in place to protect your data, both digital and physical. You've learned about some typical data security operational systems, their functions, and best practices.

Hopefully you see the need to take steps to protect your business data. Having the right systems in place will reduce the risk of unnecessary headaches.

This concludes our focus on operational systems. Let's recap the ones we've covered:

- Accounting and Inventory Management
- Human Resources
- Marketing, Sales, and Customer Support
- Project Management, File Storage, and Communication
- Data Security

In the next phase, we'll dive into standard tools for organizing and optimizing a company's operations. Stay tuned.

Chapter Eight

Standard Tools for Organizing Operations

The Four Essential Tools of Operational Systems

We have explored ten critical areas of business, laying the foundation with actionable steps and best practices for building a strong operational framework. Now, we turn our attention to four essential tools which are key to organizing and sustaining efficient operations: organizational charts, workflow charts, operations manuals, and employee handbooks. These serve as the backbone for maintaining clarity and consistency within a company.

In this chapter, we'll examine what each one is, and how it can be used best, then outline the steps for creating them. With these tools in hand, you'll be well-equipped to take operations to the next level.

Organizational Charts

The organizational chart, often called an org chart, illustrates a company's structure, visually depicting the hierarchy of departments, positions, and roles, and the ways they are each connected. It is then easy to see how authority flows, answering the important question of who reports to whom. The chart clarifies relationships between employees, teams, and management, and provides a basic understanding of everyone's responsibilities.

There are different types of org charts, including hierarchical (top-down), matrix (dual reporting lines), flat (minimal hierarchy), and three-legged stool. They can be created with staff members or functions in mind initially.

- *Hierarchical Organizational Charts:* These are pyramid shaped charts with the highest positions of authority at the top, and lower levels displayed downward, often resulting in a lengthy chain of command. Orders flow down and information for decision making flows up. An example could be the CEO on top, followed by executives, then department heads, and finally individual team members.

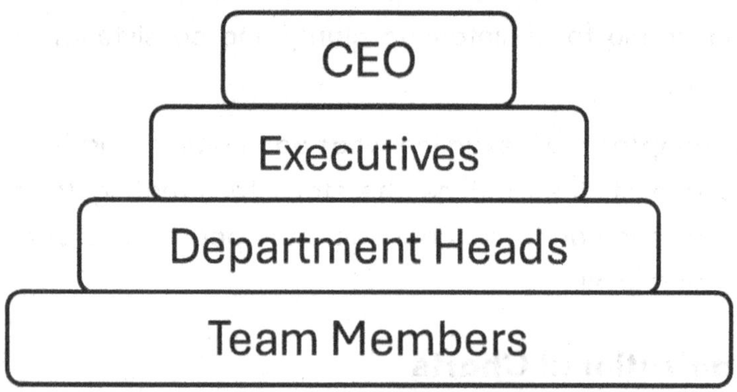

- *Matrix Organizational Charts:* These charts are often temporary, created for completing a specific project. In a matrix chart there are multiple chains of command providing cross-functional collaboration. Team members report to their department head, as in the hierarchical structure, but they also report to project managers when assigned to a project. This allows employees to remain in the traditional structure for chain of command but also gives them the freedom to collaborate across departments to achieve a larger goal for the business.

  For example, a company implementing a new CRM may want to include input from IT, sales, and finance. Pulling personnel from these departments will capture all aspects of the new software deployment while keeping people in their lanes for the company as a whole. This provides faster decision making, supports innovation and knowledge sharing, and encourages collaboration. The downside can be confusion around who employees report to, and who has final authority on decisions. To avoid this pitfall, it's essential for management to clearly define reporting lines, expectations, and decision makers from the beginning of the project. This is especially the case when team members participate in multiple projects with different managers.

Sample Matrix Org Chart

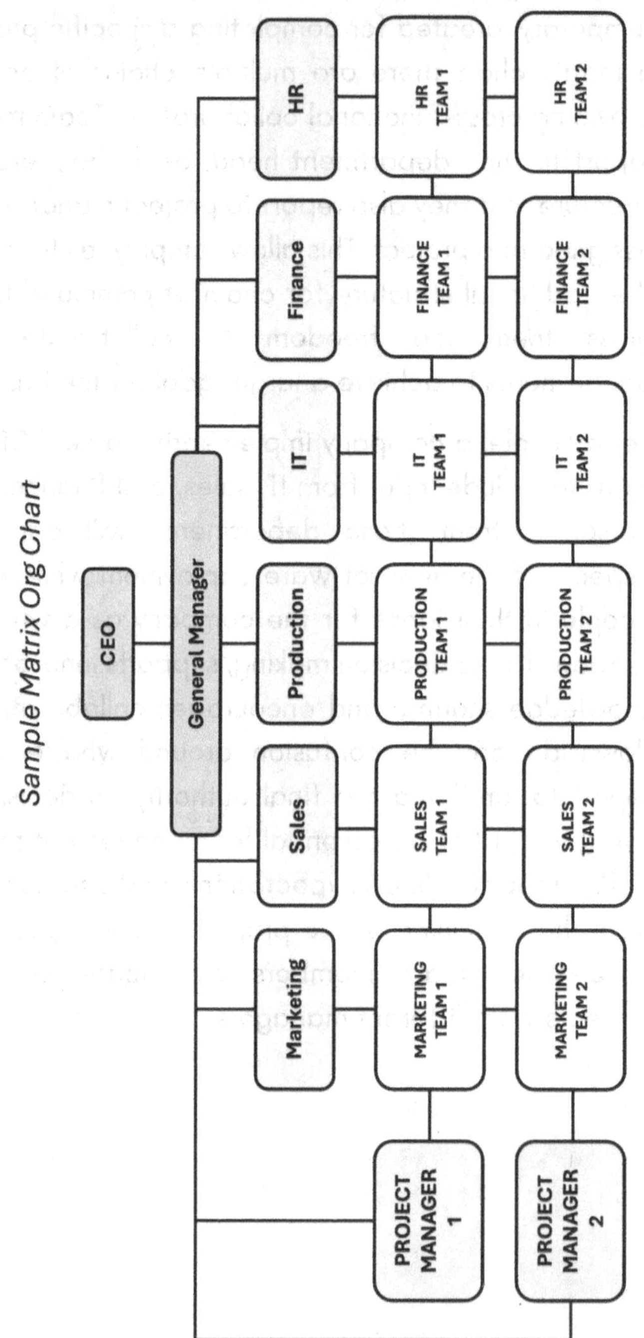

- *Flat Organizational Charts:* Unlike the hierarchical type, a flat organizational chart has few or no levels of management. It could be as streamlined as everyone in the company reporting to the CEO, or the CEO having multiple direct reports, each with a team of their own. This can be optimal for a small business needing to adapt to urgent challenges. With fewer layers of management, decisions can be made quickly, and closer to the point of impact. However, a flat organizational chart can also imply that all employees have the same authority, making it difficult to define accountability.

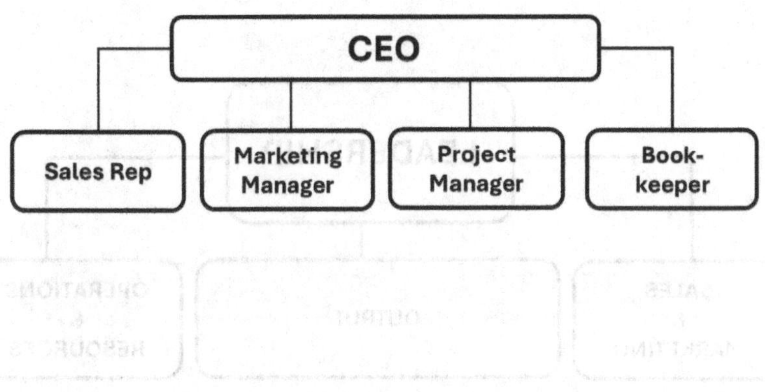

- *Three-Legged Stool Organizational Charts:* Another way of looking at an organization is as a three-legged stool: Output, Sales & Marketing, and Operations & Resources.

  Every business must have something to sell. That is the company's Output. The Sales & Marketing leg of the stool is responsible for informing the company's target audience of its products and services, and helping customers make a decision to buy. The myriad of support needs such as processes, procedures, HR, IT, facilities, and more are handled by Operations & Resources.

  A three-legged stool organizational chart can be simple or significantly large and complex, depending on the size and needs of the company.

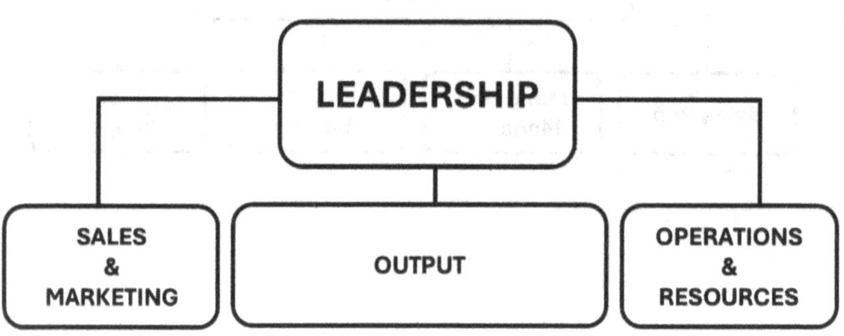

Three-Legged Stool Organizational Chart Example

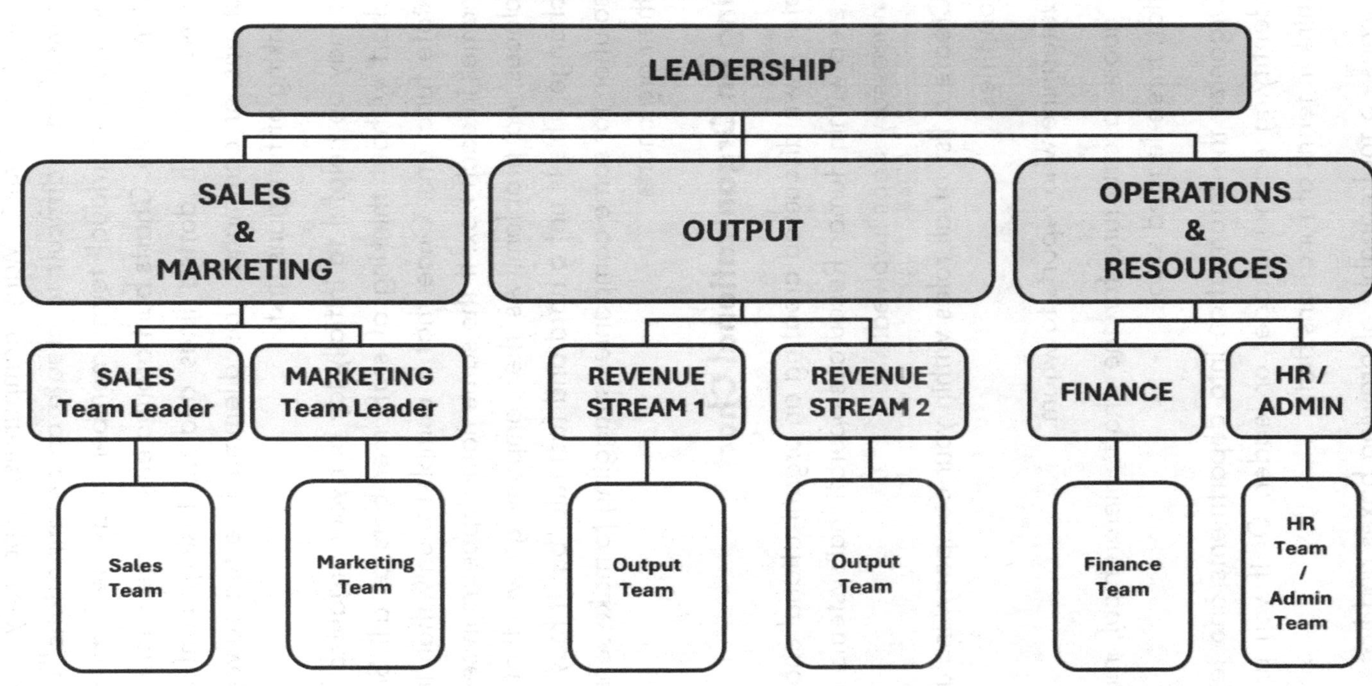

- *Functions First?:* Many companies, especially smaller firms, find it difficult to create an organizational chart, because individual team members may perform more than one role. Charts built around employees' names can wind up with dotted lines and confusing, conflicting chains of command. This dilemma is often solved by thinking of functions first.

  It may be helpful to initially lay out your organizational chart without thinking of staff members at all. Simply state functions. Once that is complete, only then insert names in each box. If the same name appears in several places, no problem. As the company grows, that can change. This is not a hard and fast rule, but it may be a solution for some companies struggling to make sense of their org charts.

Creating an Organizational Chart

In Chapter 4 we discussed creating an organizational chart as a basic step within Human Resources operational systems. Here are the necessary steps involved:

- Create a list of all roles within your company, including job titles.
- Determine who reports to whom.
- Choose a structure for the chart: hierarchical, matrix, flat, three-legged stool.
- Organize the information into departments and teams, identifying each manager or leader. Or if you prefer, think in terms of functions first.
- Choose a tool capable of drawing boxes and lines. This could be as simple as a pad of paper and a pen, or as

elaborate as a page layout program, PowerPoint, or dedicated org chart creation software.

- Create the chart by laying out where every person and/or function fits into your chosen structure.

Workflow Charts

A workflow chart is a visual representation of a process designed to achieve a desired outcome. Similar to the organizational chart, it uses symbols such as boxes and connectors. However, where the org chart is about "Who," this is about the "What." What needs to happen to get the work done and in what order? A workflow chart may also indicate the people involved, but that is not the chart's focus.

Workflow charts have specific starting and ending points, and show every step which needs to be taken in between. And remember, you're only concerned with the "What" when creating a workflow chart, not the "How." (The "How" will be spelled out in Standard Operating Procedures, discussed later in this chapter.)

Every business should have more than one workflow chart—probably several. An initial chart could depict the complete customer lifecycle, including steps such as lead, sale, fulfillment, payment, and staying connected for repeat business. Workflow charts can also be developed for individual departments, showing how projects come to the department, are handled within it, and moved to the next part of the company. Again, be sure to keep the emphasis only on what needs to be done, not how.

Key Components for Workflow Charts

When creating workflow charts, be sure to include each of these key components:

- *Start and End Points:* Use a linear diagram to identify what triggers the beginning of a workflow, and how the workflow is completed.
- *Connectors:* Use arrows to show the direction of each step. One line can wrap to another line below it if the workflow extends across an entire page.
- *Decisions:* Indicate points in the workflow where decisions are made and by whom.
- *Symbols:* Use a variety of shapes to differentiate portions of the workflow, such as start and end points, decisions (mentioned above), specific types of steps, and others.
- *Colors:* Colors can be used to identify stages, phases, or departments.

Benefits of Workflow Charts

Workflow charts provide clarity through the visual representation of everything involved in a project. Bottlenecks, redundancies, and unnecessary steps come to light, creating opportunities to improve efficiency. The charts become a standard for everyone to follow. Team members will understand where they fit into the process, resulting in collaboration and better communication.

Steps for Creating a Workflow Chart

- Define the purpose of the chart.
- List all the steps from beginning to end that must happen to complete the workflow. Capture only what needs to be done, not how it will be done.
- Identify who needs to complete each step.
- Choose a workflow creation tool with the capacity for colors, symbols, and connectors. Many software programs are available, or a workflow can be developed simply on paper, using a variety of markers, and a stencil for shapes.
- Lay out each step in the process, identifying start and end points, segments, decision markers, and who takes each step.
- Review for any inefficiencies and modify the chart accordingly.

Examples of Workflow Charts

On the next page is a simplified example of a companywide workflow chart, showing all the internal and external steps involved in the process of acquiring, serving, and retaining a client. You determine the level of detail needed within your organization.

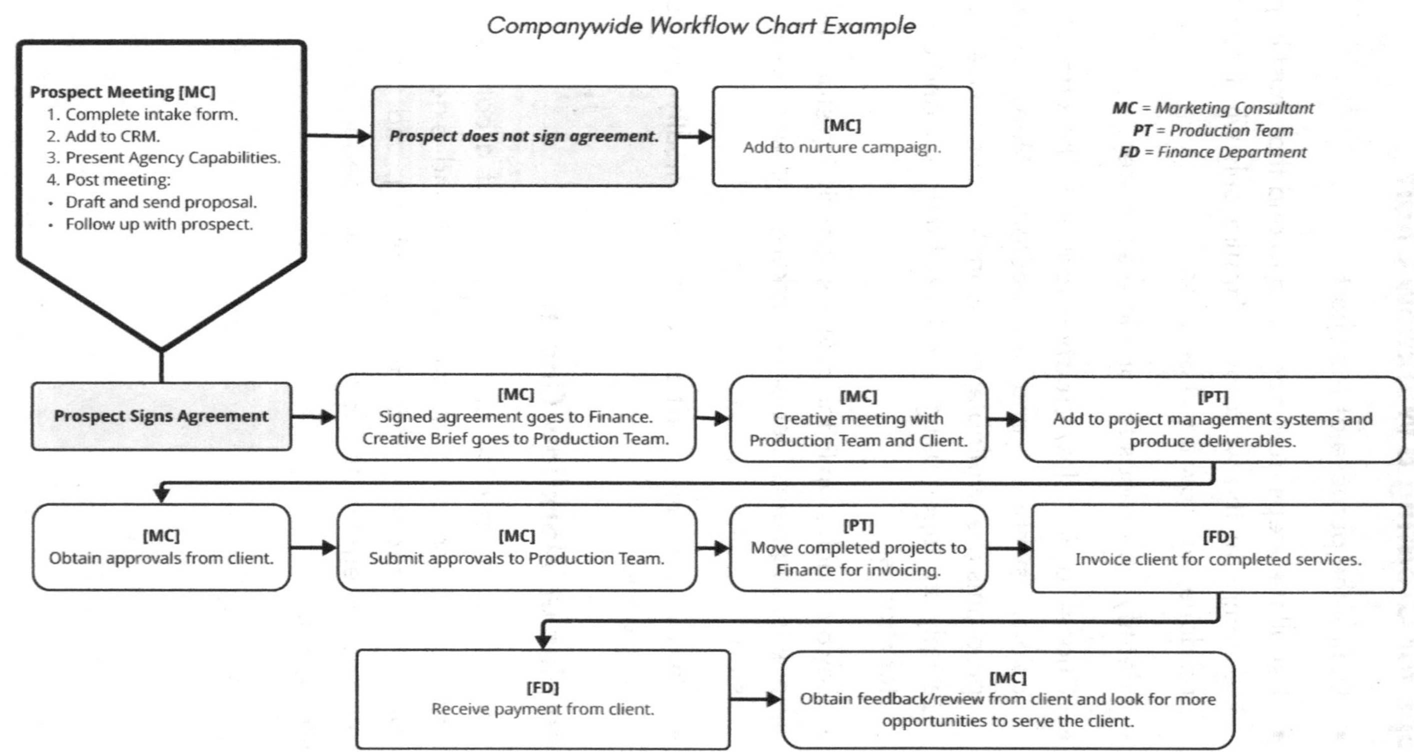
Companywide Workflow Chart Example
Prospect Meeting [MC]
1. Complete intake form.
2. Add to CRM.
3. Present Agency Capabilities.
4. Post meeting:
· Draft and send proposal.
· Follow up with prospect.
Prospect does not sign agreement.
[MC]
Add to nurture campaign.
MC = Marketing Consultant
PT = Production Team
FD = Finance Department
Prospect Signs Agreement
[MC]
Signed agreement goes to Finance.
Creative Brief goes to Production Team.
[MC]
Creative meeting with
Production Team and Client.
[PT]
Add to project management systems and
produce deliverables.
[MC]
Obtain approvals from client.
[MC]
Submit approvals to Production Team.
[PT]
Move completed projects to
Finance for invoicing.
[FD]
Invoice client for completed services.
[FD]
Receive payment from client.
[MC]
Obtain feedback/review from client and look for more
opportunities to serve the client.

On the next page is a simplified example of a department specific workflow chart, showing the company's recruitment process whenever an employment opportunity opens requiring a new hire. You determine the level of detail needed within your organization.

Department Specific Workflow Chart Example

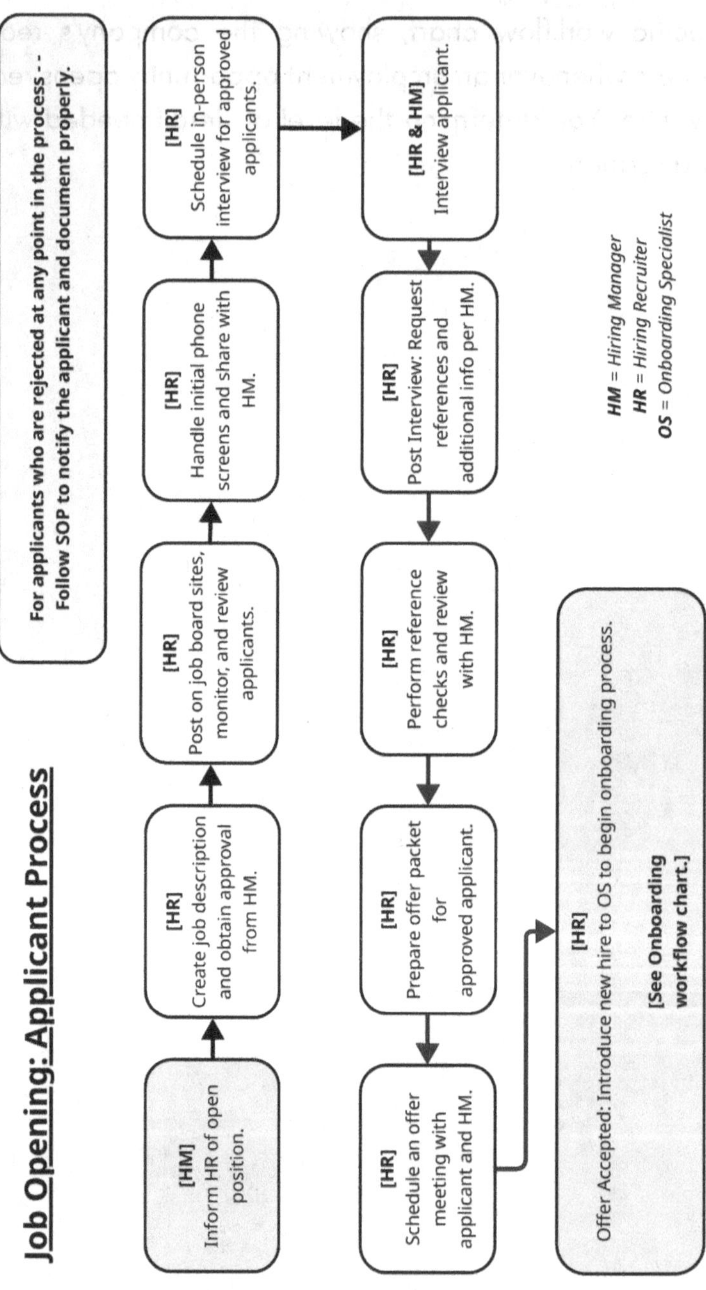

Operations Manuals (SOPS)

An operations manual is a collection of documents known as Standard Operating Procedures, or SOPs, which are written instructions detailing how to perform steps in a workflow process. The operations manual is the last piece necessary for a business to organize its workflows.

SOPs keep everyone on the same page, eliminating guesswork and minimizing wasted time trying to figure out what is expected or how to complete a task. With clear instructions in place, employees know exactly how to perform their duties and the desired outcomes. Companies that document their processes properly have a huge advantage when it comes to scaling for growth.

Recommended Elements for SOPs

Although the SOPs which make up an operations manual are customizable to the needs of the business, a few key elements should be included in each one.

- *Title:* Create a title which clearly identifies the procedure being documented, along with the related department. For example, "HR SOP - Creating A Job Description."
- *Purpose:* Outline the purpose of the SOP. "This SOP will outline the steps for creating a role description and obtaining approvals to ensure consistency, accuracy, and compliance with company policies prior to posting on job boards."
- *Scope:* Specify where, when, and to whom this SOP applies. "This procedure applies to HR Recruiters working on behalf of ABC Company who are creating job descriptions for open positions based on input from

leadership. It is to be followed prior to posting positions on job boards."

- *Responsibilities:* Indicate who is responsible for completing and overseeing the procedure.
- *Definitions:* Provide definitions of company or industry specific terms or jargon used in the document.
- *Prerequisites:* List anything needed before the steps in the SOP can be performed, such as tools, equipment, materials, permissions, etc.
- *Procedure Steps:* This is the meat of the SOP. Provide detailed step by step instructions in clear, logical order. Include images or diagrams.
- *Standards:* Explain any requirements for compliance with company or industry protocols, guidelines, and standards.
- *References:* Include links or citations for related materials to support the instructions for the procedure. This could be an SOP which precedes this step, a separate document explaining a particular company standard, etc.
- *Precautions:* Include safety protocols relevant to the procedure.
- *Approvals:* State the approvals required for any part of the procedure and utilize a date stamp requiring a signature to indicate who approved the documented process.
- *Appendices:* Direct employees to any supplemental information such as forms, checklists, and templates relevant to the procedure.

- *Version:* Provide a date stamp to indicate when the procedure was last updated. This will help eliminate the use of outdated versions, as it is important for everyone to be working from the most recent SOPs.
- *Troubleshooting:* Provide instructions on what to do if someone runs into a problem performing steps in the procedure.

Creating and Storing SOP Documentation

There are a variety of options for creating and storing the SOPs within an operations manual. Below are a few possibilities. Major objectives are to protect the documents from unauthorized revisions and make them easily accessible to necessary team members.

- *Microsoft Word, PDFs, Shared Folders:* SOPs can be created easily using Microsoft Word, then converted to .PDF files and made available to the team in a shared folder. Protect original Word documents with a password to keep them from being inadvertently changed, and store them in a separate folder accessible only to management, making them less likely to be accidentally deleted.
- *OneNote:* SOPs written in Microsoft OneNote can be shared in Microsoft TEAMS. While this is a simple format for organization and sharing, there are risks to having the information easily editable. Lock the OneNote so only management has permission to make changes, allowing the rest of the team to view them only. Backup the OneNote file whenever revisions are made.
- *Google Sites:* This option creates a user-friendly internet-based interface for accessing information. It behaves like

a website, making it easy to navigate. Google Sites is included in Google Workspace subscriptions.

Basic SOP Sample

On the next page is an example of an SOP a company might use for processing customer refunds. This sample shows basic instructions, but SOPs can get as granular as a company needs for accuracy and consistency throughout the organization. Certain steps may require additional instructions, which could be done with links to short explainer videos or screenshots.

If the SOP uses third party software, list the software version within the SOP. Should it be updated to a newer version, the relevant instructions and screenshots within the SOP may need to be revised.

Basic SOP Sample

Title: Client Services – Processing Customer Refunds
Effective Date: February 18, 2025
Last Reviewed Date: January 15, 2026
Reviewed By: Sandy Hill, Client Services Manager
Business Name: Company

---

1. Purpose
Steps for customer refunds ensuring consistency with company policies.
2. Scope
Applies to all team members who handle refund requests for online purchases.
3. Responsibilities

- Customer Service Representatives (CSRs): Initiate refund requests.
- Finance Team: Approve and process refunds.

4. Definitions

- CSR: Customer Service Representative
- Refund ID: Unique identifier assigned to each refund request

5. Prerequisites

- Access to the refund management system.
- Customer's order number and proof of purchase.

6. Procedure Steps

1. Log in to the refund management system.
2. Search for the customer's order using the order number.
3. Verify the purchase details and ensure eligibility for a refund.
4. Submit the refund request with required documentation.
5. Notify the customer of the refund status via email.

7. Standards

- Refund requests must be processed within 48 hours of submission.
- All customer communications should follow the company's email template.

8. References

- Refund Policy (Document ID: RP-2025)
- Customer Service Handbook

9. Troubleshooting

- If the refund system is down, submit the request manually using Form XYZ.
- For complex cases, escalate to the Finance Manager.

Approved By: Sandy Hill, Client Services Manager **Signature:** Sandy Hill **Date:** February 18, 2025	**Appendices** • Refund Request Form (Template) • Customer Communication Checklist

Employee Handbook for Company Policies

The employee handbook is essential for any company with a staff. Even small teams benefit from having a written handbook, creating a central place for communicating policies and culture, reducing misunderstandings, and laying a foundation for HR operations. The handbook should establish clear expectations and protect the company by covering all legal requirements. This tool sets the tone for new hires, as well as providing reference material throughout employment.

Key Elements of an Employee Handbook

An employee handbook typically includes the following key elements:

- *Introduction:* The handbook begins with a welcome message from the company, stating the handbook's purpose, and underscoring the firm's mission, vision, and values. If applicable at your location, the introduction section should include an Employment At Will disclaimer to protect both employer and employee from entering their work relationship with a wrong understanding. This establishes that either party can terminate the employment at any time for any reason without prior notice as long as no laws were violated.
- *Employment Policies:* Include policies which comply with state and federal guidelines such as anti-discrimination and harassment, equal employment opportunity, OSHA requirements, etc. Check with a professional to incorporate policies required by all entities, government and otherwise, to which your company and industry are subject.

- *Workplace Expectations and Conduct:* The contents of this section will vary, depending on the company's desired culture and expectations. Outline acceptable and non-acceptable workplace conduct, and the level of professionalism expected from employees. Examples could be policies regarding dress code, attendance, requesting and receiving approval for time off, social media and other technology usage during the workday, and more—anything important to the company related to employee behavior.
- *Compensation and Benefits:* Here team members will find information regarding how they are paid, and the employee benefits available to them. Include details such as the company policy on overtime, payday schedule, method of payment such as check or direct deposit. In addition to the common health insurance and/or retirement benefits, etc., highlight perks unique to working for your company such as continuing education or wellness programs.
- *Work Hours and Leave Policies:* Unlike the Workplace Expectations and Conduct section (see above), which touched on time off requests and approvals, this section details what is available to the employee for vacation, PTO, sick or family leave, etc. Include defined work hours and remote employment policies. These can be role specific as needed. For example, a sales position may require remote work at times, while a front desk receptionist role may be in office only.
- *Performance and Growth:* Employees expect to have performance evaluations. These are best when connected to career advancement opportunities

whenever possible. Explain how evaluations are handled, outline career paths specific to each role, and describe any training and continuing education policies. For example, does the company pay for a portion of training costs, or is the employee solely responsible? Be sure to follow each policy consistently with every employee.

- *Disciplinary and Termination Policies:* Unfortunately, not every hire works out. An organization needs a procedure for managing any employee who does not comply with company policies or meet with the position's requirements. This section should cover specifics on what will trigger disciplinary action, and a progressive approach to resolving poor performance. This is also where employees will find details for the termination process, whether voluntary or involuntary.
- *Confidentiality and Data Protection:* State details concerning protection of company assets and proprietary information. If the company requires confidentiality agreements, disclose that here. We touched on technology usage in the Workplace Expectations and Conduct paragraph, above. Expand upon company technology, cybersecurity, and data protection policies in this section of your employee handbook.
- *Acknowledgment and Agreement:* Conclude with a form acknowledging the employee's receipt and understanding of the handbook. This should be signed at the start of employment and any time updates are made to the book during employment.

Final Thoughts on Employee Handbooks

If you choose to write the employee handbook internally, make sure to have it reviewed by an HR professional who knows the legal requirements of government and your industry. Have any future edits reviewed as well. This will protect the organization from potential lawsuits which could result from an employee complaint.

Standard Tools for Organizing Operations - Conclusion

These four essential tools—organizational charts, workflow charts, operations manuals (SOPs), and employee handbooks—create a structured foundation for business operations. Each one plays a crucial role in maintaining clarity, consistency, and accountability, ensuring that employees understand their roles, workflows are streamlined, procedures are documented, and company policies are clear. When used together, these tools create a well-organized workplace supporting productivity and growth. Your business will be better equipped to adapt, scale, and maintain a strong company culture.

To help you quickly identify when and why to implement these foundational tools, the chart below offers a simplified reference. Use it as a guide to prioritize what to create now and what to prepare for as your business grows.

Tool	When It's Needed	Why It's Important
Org Chart	When you're ready to delegate duties to employees or contractors.	Clarifies roles, responsibilities, and reporting structure to support a well-organized team.
Workflow Chart	As your processes become more defined and you're preparing to add team members.	Helps visualize how work flows through your business; useful for training and identifying inefficiencies.
SOPs (Standard Operating Procedures)	When you're moving from solo operations to a more structured system, ideally *before* hiring.	Ensures consistency, clarity, and smooth onboarding as you bring others into your operations.
Employee Handbook	When you're ready to hire employees or build a team.	Establishes clear expectations, outlines policies, and protects both the business and team members.

Chapter Nine

From Vision to Execution

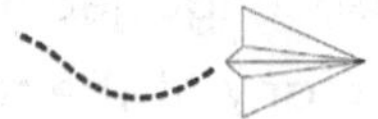

Your New Reality

At the start of this book, we envisioned a future where your business runs seamlessly, free of bottlenecks and inefficiencies, at full potential. Since then, we've guided you through business operations broken into ten categories, explaining each component, outlining strategies, and providing actionable tasks to implement. We even dedicated a chapter to essential foundational tools. If you apply what you've learned, that future isn't just a possibility, it is becoming your reality.

Let's Revisit JB Marketing

Remember JB Marketing, the fictional company we introduced at the beginning of our journey through operational systems? Their owner, James Bean, took action, implementing the best practices found in this book. As a result, business is thriving, and James couldn't be more pleased. Let's take a closer look.

- *Accounting:* James transitioned from using Microsoft Excel and Word for accounting to a QuickBooks setup. This enabled the company to centralize bookkeeping tasks, automate recurring services, and reduce manual data entry. Offering automatic payments made transactions more convenient for clients, and increased the percentage of timely receivables, improving cash flow.

Streamlined categorizations of income and expenses now provide clearer insights into profit and loss data, making financial reports much more beneficial than before. James also engaged an external bookkeeping service to handle many of the tasks so he could focus on what he does best—providing marketing services for clients.

- *Communication:* JB Marketing's previous methods of communication were Google Workspace tools such as Email, Chat, and Meet for the internal team, plus Zoom and in-person appointments with clients. Although there were no obvious pain points when James started his search for improvements, he did learn some tips to enhance communication. For example, he implemented a video screen sharing program for training purposes. This has significantly reduced internal meetings. James can now create detailed instructions for any project or process. Team members reference them as needed, leading to enhanced efficiency. Along the way, James discovered AI tools for capturing notes during calls and providing summaries to participants. These reduce post-meeting administrative tasks.
- *Project Management and CRM (Customer Relationship Management):* Regarding project management, James initially used a free platform which lacked CRM capabilities and multi-user access, requiring him to track all tasks himself. Client information was stored in his personal Google Contacts, limiting accessibility to the team. Recurring service details, including descriptions

and fees, were tracked in spreadsheets, while customer emails were organized in Gmail folders.

Upgrading to a paid platform with both CRM and project management features significantly improved JB Marketing's workflow. The new system enables better task tracking, collaboration, client data management, and timely project completion. By integrating project management with the CRM, James streamlined JB Marketing's sales pipeline. Although Google Contacts is still used for quick access, the CRM efficiently tracks sales efforts, creating smoother client engagement.

- *Customer Support:* In the past, James was the sole point of contact for clients, managing all communications via his cell phone and email. As the client base grew, he found it increasingly difficult to maintain a high level of service.

  The first step toward resolving this was hiring an assistant. For telephone support, JB Marketing implemented an app which provides each team member, including James, a unique business phone number. When unavailable, he can easily forward calls to his assistant. An email address dedicated to production topics enables prompt responses to client communications and faster resolution of issues. These changes allow JB Marketing to maintain excellent customer service as revenues increase.

- *File Management:* Previously, digital files were stored in a folder system within James' personal Google Drive account, then forwarded via email to staff members. Switching to shared drives organized by department with clear folder structures eliminated delays caused by inefficient file access. With this new system, supported by SOPs, team members can find necessary files quickly. Productivity and collaboration have improved as a result.

- *HRMS (Human Resources):* James originally ran JB Marketing as a sole proprietor, managing a team of independent contractors, while handling all customer support and working against deadlines—an overwhelming balancing act. By hiring employees as needed and building an organizational chart, James now shares these burdens, giving him greater capacity to grow the business. Newly implemented workflow charts have set the stage for bringing all services in house eventually, to allow more control even with a larger staff.
- *Inventory Management:* The only tangible inventory at JB Marketing are office supplies. Although initially overlooked, James recognized the importance of tracking these when the business grew. An Excel spreadsheet created for inventory management combined with a recurring audit reduced unnecessary purchases and streamlined ordering. Supplies are now replenished timely without overstocking.
- *Marketing and Sales:* JB Marketing already had an excellent website and sent an eblast to clients and prospects regularly, but James took care of Search Engine Optimization (SEO) and social media efforts himself rather haphazardly. By delegating these tasks to an independent contractor with a clear marketing budget and a 12-month plan, inbound leads increased by 25%. This has the potential for even greater growth in the coming year, as it allows for more strategic use of marketing resources.

- *Security and Data Backup:* JB Marketing's security and data backup have always been adequately managed by an IT firm. However, James faced disruptions when his sole internet service provider experienced downtime, affecting the ability to serve clients and communicate among the team. Investing in a secondary service for internet access means zero outages. This solution enhances reliability and keeps projects moving, with the added benefit of solid client trust.

These are just a few highlights of the operational improvements implemented at our fictitious company, JB Marketing. James now sees positive impacts across the board. He's committed to making ongoing adjustments with business operations as a key driver so he can focus on the quality of service his company provides. Each change has streamlined operations, reduced delays, enhanced service, and improved resource management, all contributing to the company's success. We can expect JB Marketing to gain greater brand recognition as a highly sought-after agency.

Final Thoughts

Where does your business stand today? Have you begun applying what you've learned in these pages? If not, it's not too late. Knowledge alone is valuable, but execution is what drives real progress. I encourage you to keep this book as your guide to continue taking action. You'll soon enjoy the rewards of a more efficient, profitable company, thanks to the advantage of operational systems.

About the Author

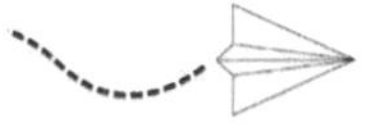

With over 20 years' experience in corporate administration and operations, Tonya Odio founded Executive Foundations with the mission to help business owners streamline their systems and build companies that profit through operational efficiency. She brings a practical approach, offering actionable strategies which reduce overwhelm and free up time for what matters most.

Tonya enjoys working with entrepreneurs, creating systems and structures to help their businesses thrive. She finds deep fulfillment in seeing organizations become well-organized, leading to improvements in the bottom line.

Family and friends are Tonya's top priorities outside her professional life, along with exploring Florida's beaches and local restaurants, or watching a good movie. And one of her core values is "fun", because life is simply better when you're enjoying it.

www.ingramcontent.com/pod-product-compliance
Lightning Source LLC
LaVergne TN
LVHW031338150826
845673LV00012B/2945

* 9 7 9 8 9 9 8 6 6 1 0 2 0 *